AF413468

OVER THE
SHOULDER

OVER THE SHOULDER

A Freelancer's Guide to Telling Stories and Editing Films

Mark Solomon

Editor: *Shark Tale, Chicken Run, Frankenweenie*
Eddie Nominee: Best Edited Animated Feature Film

7 Pines Publishing

To NVH,

For all your inspiration

CONTENTS

Preview[1]

Long ago in a galaxy called New York City, I auditioned for a quirky theatre project devoted to traditional Asian drama. For a young actor, this became a welcome gig: a summer in Connecticut with room and board, and maybe a good story to tell.

Our teachers and directors were accomplished artists from Bali, India and Japan, and that summer changed my life, opening me up to a rich world of new ideas about story and drama. What makes a good villain? What does an audience consider beautiful? Funny? Frightening? These questions popped and fizzed in my mind for months and years.

I couldn't get enough of the Japanese plays and their refined aesthetic. I read everything I could about Noh, Kabuki and Kyogen theatre. The essentials I learned that summer had a major impact on my creative thinking, first as an actor and eventually as a film editor, with a career in Hollywood

---

[1] This Preview (introduction) has not yet been rated.

spanning more than 30 years, editing animated films, such as *Shrek*[2], *Chicken Run*[3], *Space Jam*[4], and *Frankenweenie*[5], nominated in 2012 for an *Eddie* award as Best Edited Animated Feature Film.

Alas, I didn't win, but as a member of a select club of nominees, I would like to share what I have learned about editing and telling stories. My purpose here is to use my experience to tilt the odds in your favor to find success in this highly competitive field.

I have been lucky to live my dream and work with some of the best A-list creative filmmakers in the business, such as Tim Burton, Mel Gibson, Nick Park, and Gary Ross. I was in the room with directors, producers, writers and composers who set the standard for stories that have resonated with a large global audience. Some were big budget productions. Others were tiny independents. Some won Oscars, and others wound up in court battles. Others are still collecting dust in a vault somewhere in the Rocky Mountains.

---

[2] *Shrek* (2001). Screenplay: William Steig, Ted Elliott, Terry Rosio. Directors: Andrew Adamson and Vicky Jensen. Editor: Sim Evan-Jones.

[3] *Chicken Run* (2000). Screenplay: Karey Kirkpatrick. Directors: Peter Lord and Nick Park. **Editor: Yours Truly**.

[4] *Space Jam* (1996). Screenplay: Leo Benvenuti, Steve Rudnick, Timothy Harris, Herschel Weingrod. Director: Joe Pytka. Editor: Sheldon Kahn.

[5] *Frankenweenie* (2012). Screenplay: Leonard Ripps, Tim Burton, John August. Director: Tim Burton. Editors: Chris Lebenzon and Yours Truly.

Over the Shoulder is literally how I learned, watching expert editors at work. If I was lucky, this meant working with a visionary who liked to talk, whose creative process benefitted from having someone like me nearby, eager to learn, who could be called on to serve as instant audience to test a new idea.

IT TAKES A VILLAGE

Producing any creative work for the screen, like a movie, a streaming series or even a short reel on your phone, means the story is told three times. First by the screenwriter with words on the page, then by the director and actors making a screenplay come alive, and then by the editor, who brings together all the visuals and sound in the most dynamic way possible.

As Orson Welles once said, "The notion of directing a film is the invention of critics. The whole eloquence of cinema is achieved in the editing room."

It's a team effort to fulfill or exceed the original vision of the writer, to breathe life into the story. In the end, a film relies on cameras, lighting, costumes, and actors bringing their experience and craft to the job at hand—and the way an editor brings them all together.

"The film is made in the editing room," said Philip Seymour Hoffman. "The shooting of the film is about shopping, almost. It's like going to get all the ingredients together, and you've got to make sure before you leave the store that you got all the ingredients. And then you take those ingredients, and you can make a good cake . . . or not."

As for the editor, no matter how fast A.I. technology disrupts the process, secrets continue to be passed down from old masters to new students on naming the tools, why they are effective and how best to use them to produce an emotional, memorable result. These tricks of the trade were shared with me, and I am passing them on to you here.

We will explore contrast, cause and effect, suspense and surprise, along with little-known principles from the Japanese stage that make a visual story pop. These tools can seduce your audience into a conversation, and guide your decisions in whatever medium you choose, whether you're writing a novel, working on a screenplay or pitching a new startup to investors.

All these tools exist to tell a compelling story. No matter what medium you work in, your story is everything. Some books about visual storytelling present the creative process as a mysterious, bubbling stew of 'feel' and 'rhythm' that depends on inspired whispers from your muse. Others want you to believe it's a cut and dry, button-pushing exercise, where powerful editing software rules all and if you know what buttons to push, you can call yourself an editor, a director, or heaven help us, a creative executive.

PERSPECTIVE

In a visual story, *over the shoulder* indicates a shot composed with two characters, allowing the viewer to see the facial expressions of one character and the physical distance between them and their scene partner. The camera typically shoots from behind the character in the foreground while holding both characters in frame. It offers a point of view that provides intimate detail while allowing viewers to see how the two characters share a common space.

Over the shoulder also suggests the keen eye of observation, such as when one of your parents stands behind you and checks to see if you are doing your homework or sneaking a peek at Netflix. Nice try. They'll catch you most of the time, as mine did when I couldn't resist watching *Ultraman* when I was meant to be solving math problems instead.

If you are hungry to learn the tools needed to tell an unforgettable story that evokes tears and laughter, or if you want to support yourself with freelance work and claim the true value of what you bring to the table, then this book is for you. If you want to create online content that has emotional resonance, keep reading. Or if you just want to tell better bedtime stories to your kids, you will find something here for you, too.

I invite you to take a seat over my shoulder. That's what I wanted when I started out, from my academic advisors at university to the editors who took a chance and hired me. They let me in on a secret, took me into their confidence, and let me see how they did their magic.

The climate is different today, largely due to the unintended consequence of working in a digital environment. The technology that brings us together has become a barrier that keeps us apart. Everyone sits at their own workstation and casual conversations overheard in the hallway have disappeared. There's less opportunity to sit together and watch a scene come alive in the edit. As a result, passing on the craft of storytelling had been compromised, a sacrifice to the speed and efficiency of digital workspaces.

We adapt, as any wily artist must do. So, let's agree on some ground rules. I'm not sharing what I know for an ego boost. I come to this sincerely. I assume you are, too, and will take what you find useful to tell your story. It can be a true story or a fantasy, a bedtime tale, a manifesto or even a eulogy, as long as you endeavor to make your story shine. I encourage you to use the secrets and "inside baseball" I am offering here to make something meaningful.

If even one idea sharpens your instincts and makes your story shine, then it's worth your time and mine. All I ask is that you use what I am offering, What happens if you don't? If you let your story die on the vine, you will pay a price when you look in the mirror. I know this from experience. No kidding? Don't thank me. Just do it. Tell your story.

Let's make an agreement, so there's no confusion. On the next page, you can sign your end of the deal and send a copy to me, care of my website, listed in the back. I'll post it and we can share accountability!

OUR AGREEMENT

I, Mark Solomon, the author of this book, agree to share what I know about film editing and storytelling. I will be as generous and honest as I possibly can. I will share my personal story, the interior life of a film editor, and the exterior life of working in the movie business. All I ask in return is that you, the reader, will read it and use it!

____

Author

I, the reader of this book, agree to read what Mark knows about film editing and storytelling. I will be as open and focused as I possibly can.

I will absorb Mark's personal story, the interior life of a film editor, and the exterior life of working in the movie business. All I ask in return is that Mark, the author, responds when I write to him!

Reader

PAYING IT FORWARD

Why a formal agreement? I do it for Ted Kloos and Wendell Phillips, the teachers who kindled my love for theatre and the performing arts; for Victor Nord and Manuel Lutgenhorst, for understanding dramatic writing and visual design; for Tony Gibbs and Rob Kobrin, editors who gave me my first break.

I owe so much to these "ancestors," the artists and teachers who took time to share what they considered worthwhile because they trusted me to do something with it. They let me sit over their shoulder, and now they encourage me to pass on what they thought I could use as a willing pupil, eager to learn how to move people with a story. They trusted me with knowledge they shared and now I am paying that forward with you.

This book offers a shortcut to storytelling insights that can take years to figure out. Think of me as your uncle in the movie business, but not the wacko at a family barbecue. I'm your ally without an agenda who just wants you to succeed. This is your chance to learn the craft of storytelling, practical matters of freelance work and how to create and maintain a work/life balance to keep yourself healthy and strong.

When a student sits over a teacher's shoulder to observe a demonstration, or a teacher looks over a student's shoulder to check their work, an unspoken, intimate agreement honors their one-to-one communication. Certain truths are whispered in these moments, as Tibetan monks would say, and that's a big inspiration for the title.

So, here we go. Imagine you're sitting over my shoulder when the usual frantic pace of the cutting room slows down and we can talk about the big questions of taking a good story and making it great, along with other subjects that inform who we are.

Do you read me? I hope you will find this book valuable, and that you will use these tools and care for them as I have done throughout my career. Give them a chance. See which nuggets spark your imagination and then you can determine which ones are right for you to keep and cultivate as your own.

Good luck!

REEL 1

Facing the Screen

Facing the Screen

As I mentioned in the Preview, my summer theatre experience as a young actor left a lasting impression on me as a storyteller.

In the West, a live performance begins with a cue from the stage manager, who sits in a booth behind the seats. The cue goes to the technicians, who darken the theatre, open the curtain, and bring up the lights. The actors take their places offstage, and on cue they enter and begin the play.

In Japan, traditional Noh theatre goes about things in a more refined way. The actors stand behind a small curtain in a corner of the stage, listening for the audience chatter to die down. They wait until everyone is quiet and ready for the show to begin. Then, they wait a little longer until a nervous feeling goes through the crowd that something must be wrong. Why haven't they started?!

They wait a little longer. What's happening? Somebody *do* something! Then, and only then, when all eyes are riveted on the stage, the lead actor gives the command to open the curtain, "Omaku," and the actors enter. As they approach center stage, they listen for the audience's breathing and align their own breaths with the general rhythm. Over the course of the play, they will take charge of that rhythm and lead the audience to a crescendo at the climax of the story. This is a moment of unfolding we will talk about later in REEL Two.

From the start, the actors engage the audience in a conversation. We are ready to start the play. Why are they waiting? A little longer. Is something wrong?

The audience is engaged from the very first moment.

Without realizing it, they have unwittingly agreed to converse with the performers and engage with the drama unfolding. The table is set to tell a riveting story.

AN UNSPOKEN CONTRACT

There's always an unspoken contract with the audience, exchanging their attention for some benefit in entertainment, emotion, and insight. Where the cinematic experience comes alive is in the space *between* the screen and the viewer. If the action onscreen does not resonate with viewers, the images are reduced to shadows flickering across a wall in a dark room.

It's only when an audience is compelled to follow along with the story that they occupy the space between themselves and the screen. In that moment, something miraculous comes alive. The story breathes. The viewers are persuaded to move from passive receivers to active participants, and the ancient spirits live again.

"There is nothing else, just us and the cameras, and those wonderful people out there in the dark."
—Norma Desmond in *Sunset Boulevard*

13

When we watch a drama unfold through time, we carry on an inner dialogue with what's happening. Even though it's only in our heads, we decide to accept the fact that we have joined a game of mental ping pong. All good stories and drama in any medium are about sustaining a conversation with the audience. When that doesn't happen, it's a waste of everybody's time, but when it does happen, it's sublime.

The Essentials aka The Secret Sauce

A magician appears from behind the curtain, wearing a beautiful tuxedo with a sparkly cape, and his lovely assistant wears a flashy outfit and a big smile. She presents the magician with a silk top hat and the lights go down. The magician waves a cane over the upturned hat, makes some hocus pocus gestures to indicate that the magic is coming, then reaches a white-gloved hand deep into the hat and *voila!*

He pulls out . . . nothing!

There's no rabbit. A modern audience claps meekly because they see something that reminds them of a real magic trick. But they feel politely disappointed that there is no there, there. All sizzle, but no steak.

Too many films and stories remind me of a bad magic act. Does this sound familiar?

In the digital flood of content, so many stories remind me of this mediocrity. They promise the pleasures of a story well-told but fall woefully short. The experience leaves us with an empty feeling that's something's missing, but it's not easy to pin down what it is. What's worse, we've become so accustomed to this by now that nobody gets angry and throws rotten tomatoes. Times have changed. Does anyone bring rotting groceries to a theatre anymore?

CAN YOU BELIEVE IT?

Your magic trick, aka your secret sauce, is knowing the nuts and bolts of what makes an effective story work. The white gloves and silk top hat can come later.

Before we look at the "how," let's ask ourselves why. Why does a good story work? What is it that we recognize in a good story that makes it come alive?

A good story relates what happened from a clear beginning, right through the middle and up to the end. (Not necessarily in that order) But why? Why do we go along with what is essentially a big fat lie, "a fiction, a dream of passion," as Hamlet phrased it in a play so well constructed it was named after its main character? Why put our cynicism and disbelief on hold to let someone tell us some elaborate crock of bull?

The short answer is, it's a heart thing, not a head thing. In our heart of hearts, we yearn to believe. If the story being told to us contains something we can believe; if it moves us to feel something, then we will spend our time and offer our attention to hear it play out. It doesn't have to be factual, but it must ring true to *feel* true and inspire us to suspend our disbelief.

A "true" story has something of value to transmit about how it feels to be alive right now, how it feels to fall in love, how to fight, or how to solve problems, how to triumph as a queen or a hero or even an animated yellow sponge.

A good story engages the emotions and makes us feel something. If you are judged to be an able storyteller, your viewers are persuaded to let their critical guard down and allow the heart to believe it's true. In that moment, they say "Yes" to what you are offering. You're not asking them to accept that the people and events described are *real*, but only to accept that your story is worth their time because it feels true.

And that depends upon one thing . . .

THE MAGIC OF BELIEF

Once you're willing to accept the unlikely idea that Dorothy's house flies on its own to a land called Oz, where she meets a wizard, flying monkeys and a tin man, the story has won you over. (Flying monkeys, really? With little hats?)

You believe it because you are persuaded by the characters to feel for them: a dreamy young farm girl, a scarecrow with no brain, and a very silly lion. Once you feel for them and their predicaments, you're willing to skip down the yellow brick road with the story. By the end, you allow yourself to feel something emotionally resonant along with this pretend Kansas farm girl. When Dorothy says, "There's no place like home," it stirs our own feelings about home and connects with us on a deeper emotional level.

The iconic film critic, Roger Ebert, once remarked that, "*The Wizard of Oz*[6] has a wonderful surface of comedy and music … but we still watch it six decades later because its underlying story penetrates straight to the deepest insecurities of childhood, stirs them, and then reassures them."

At the time, not everyone felt that way. When the movie opened, Otis Ferguson wrote in *The New Republic* that, "It has dwarfs, Technicolor, freak characters, and Judy Garland. It can't be expected to have a sense of humor as well."

You can't please everyone.

"You've always had the power, my dear.
You just had to learn it for yourself."
—Glinda, the Good Witch from *The Wizard of Oz*

In 1939, the Academy Award for Best Picture went to *Gone With the Wind*[7] in a famously brilliant year for Hollywood moviemaking. The Oscar for Best Editing went to Ralph Dawson for *The Adventures of Robin Hood*[8]. It's a fun adventure,

---

[6] *The Wizard of Oz* (1939) Screenplay: Noah Langley, Florence Ryerson, Edgar Allan Woolf. Directors: Victor Fleming and King Vidor. Editor: Blanche Sewell.

[7] *Gone With the Wind* (1939) Screenplay: Margaret Mitchell, Sidney Howard. Director: Victor Fleming. Editors: Hal C. Kern and James E. Newcom.

[8] *The Adventures of Robin Hood* (1938) Screenplay: Norman Reilly Raine and Seton I. Miller. Directors: Michel Curtiz and William Keighley. Editor: Ralph Dawson.

starring Errol Flynn, but not with the same enduring resonance of *The Wizard of Oz*.

So, how did they do it?

2

It's All About Conflict

Storytellers make an unspoken agreement with their audience: in exchange for their time, attention, and the cost of a movie, cable service or streaming platform, the creators "promise" to offer a worthwhile and entertaining product: something emotional, delightful, or resonant, preferably all three. Or else why bother?

It's a straightforward transaction. Holding up your end of the bargain means respecting the audience's attention by understanding why and how stories work and delivering an experience they'll never forget.

Let's start with "Why."

WHAT IS YOUR THEME,
AND WHY DOES YOUR STORY MATTER?

Why does a story merit attention? What about it sparks curiosity? Does it connect with what people are feeling and thinking today? A successful theme acts like a magnet to draw interest.

"Hey, maybe this story will teach me something about some difficulty I'm facing in my own life."

Does your theme offer an original take on a familiar idea, or is it a rehash of stories we have all heard before?

As the editor, you don't invent the initial story, so you won't need to come up with the theme, but it is vital that you can identify and articulate it in terms that guide your decisions and move the story forward.

The entire team of filmmakers, including producers, screenwriters, director, actors, crew, and *you*, the editor, contribute. The theme can be solid from the beginning, or it can evolve as the production develops, but the best themes find a way to balance the classics of human drama with the novelty of a new setting or a fresh approach.

You can help your chances of success when you describe the theme in active language. This makes the theme dynamic and leaves you free to whisper it so audiences discover it for themselves, or you can shout it from the water tower high above a Hollywood studio.

Examples of Theme:
The Godfather[9]
Among violent criminals, the bonds of family are valued above all else.

---

[9] *The Godfather* (1972) Screenplay: Mario Puzo and Francis Ford Coppola. Director: Frances Ford Coppola. Editors: William Reynolds and Peter Zinner.

Jurassic Park[10]

Human efforts to control the power of nature are doomed to fail.

Shark Tale[11]

Despite what others may say, accepting the truth about yourself takes real courage.

To think like an editor, identify and embrace the theme so that all decisions flow from a natural, unifying source. The theme is what lets you connect with the entire creative team, all working together toward a common goal. When the theme is clear, the story has a better chance to sing, but when it's murky and vague, everyone can wind up pulling in different directions and the results will suffer.

For example, when editing *Chicken Run*, the theme was clear. By working together, even silly chickens can find the courage to be free, and the story had a natural resonance.

In *The Tale of Despereaux*,[12] the story was pulled in two directions. One theme is about love and forgiveness, and another is about rising from darkness to light. The movie still has its charms, but it didn't quite jell as we had hoped.

---

[10] *Jurassic Park* (1993) Screenplay: Michael Crichton. Director: Steven Spielberg. Editor: Michael Kahn.

[11] *Shark Tale* (2004) Screenplay: Michael J. Wilson and Rob Letterman. Directors: Bibo Bergeron, Vicky Jenson, and Rob Letterman. Editors: Nick Fletcher, Peter Lonsdale, and John Venzon. Additional Editor: Yours Truly

[12] *The Tale of Despereaux* (2008) Screenplay: Kate DiCamillo, Gary Ross, Will McRobb, and Chris Viscardi. Directors: Sam Fell and Robert Stevenhagen. Editor: Yours Truly.

Let's see how this works and make up one possible scenario. Imagine the theme of our story is overcoming obstacles to self-expression. With that central idea, let's see how it can be expressed as a story and compare examples of similar stories on the same theme.

In *Chronicles*, Bob Dylan's autobiography, he tells his story of being an unknown songwriter with something to say. He trudges through a cold winter in Greenwich Village, going door to door with his guitar, trying to get someone in the music business to listen. When he is finally heard, his songs change the world.

Or what about Eminem winning a rap battle at the end of *8 Mile*[13]? As a white rapper in a Black community, most everyone believes that he does not belong. But his talent and authenticity shine through and he wins a contest to be celebrated by his peers.

Or consider *CODA*[14], about a girl from a deaf family who struggles to find her voice. Facing psychological conflicts about being the only hearing member of her deaf family, she overcomes crippling self-doubt and fear to give a successful audition at a prestigious music school.

The theme is the same—overcoming obstacles to self-expression—but it will be conveyed through the clash of opposites, which are specific and unique in each case. The

---

[13] *8 Mile* (2002) Screenplay: Scott Silver. Director: Curtis Hanson. Editors: Craig Kitson and Jay Rabinowitz.

[14] *CODA* (2021) Screenplay: Sian Heder, Victoria Bedos, and Stanislas Carré de Malberg. Director: Sian Heder. Editor: Geraud Brisson.

resisting force can come from the family or the music business or a peer group, with each creating a formidable obstacle. But the hero's goal—what they want—remains the same: to express their unique voice and be heard. Regardless of how it manifests, that conflict is the heart of drama, the next essential element of telling a good story.

A theme remains static until it is illuminated through the clash of opposites. When that happens, you have drama. Then the story starts to move.

Stanley Kubrick said it well when it comes to the power of editing: "Editing is the only unique aspect of filmmaking which does not resemble any other art form – a point so important it cannot be overstressed. It can make or break a film."

CONFLICT EQUALS DRAMA

When two opposing forces clash, we learn more about them by seeing their qualities in action. Which one is stronger? Which one is more cunning? Which one seems likely to prevail?

The conflict reveals the two sides in sharper focus and gives a sense of what's at stake. Depending on the outcome, the prize will be lost or won. The higher the value of what's at risk, the more riveted an audience will be to see what happens.

That question drives the story forward . . . relentlessly. What happens next? Or, to begin at the beginning, what happens first?

3

Is Genre a Dirty Word?

People can't help it. We naturally look for patterns to make sense of the world around us. Is this situation a danger I recognize from previous experience? Do I need to be extra cautious here? Or is it a welcome oasis, like a place I know from past revels?

Recognizing patterns is hardwired into our nervous system. Once that process has been successfully triggered, audiences enjoy predicting what type of story they're being asked to follow. They look for clues in a thousand little details: the style of clothing, the setting, how the characters move, and what catches their attention, and then viewers compare them with what they have seen before. Pattern recognition is our way of being present in the world.

Without much effort, people immediately look to create categories and ask questions.

What is this story like?

Have I seen something like this before?

How might this one be different?

As storytellers, it would be smart to play with these expectations in the unspoken dialogue you have with your audience.

Genre is how you can add spice to the conversation about what kind of story you're telling and what kind of world we are entering.

Genre gets a bad reputation because it's often mistaken to mean formulaic. A "genre picture" refers to a lesser creation, a lazy by-the-numbers recipe that exploits cheap sex, gory violence, and wooden dialogue. But it ain't necessarily so.

Genre essentially means the type of story being told, inferring a category, such as romance or adventure, a thriller, or a melodrama.

What do we know about stories like this?

What about this looks familiar?

It's no secret that we have all heard numerous stories before and have a natural sense of the directions a particular story can take. As a storyteller, you can use that instinct to your advantage. To start a story with a delicate young woman scrubbing floors, with her upturned eyes gazing out the window, we readily recall Cinderella and know where her story might lead. On the other hand, if we creep in on the window at night where she brushes her hair in the mirror, wearing a white slip while anxious violins screech on the soundtrack, you can bet that the fake blood will soon be splattering.

Genre defines the world of the story. Comedy. Drama. Action. Thriller. Romance. A longer list is available to study on any streaming service of your choice. Each genre has a different set of expectations for how the story unfolds, and how people behave within the rules for how that world operates.

As an editor, once you know the genre of your story, you can review other examples to get a clearer sense about how that world operates. What are the rules? How is this project like other stories in the same genre? How is it different?

In a musical like *Lala Land*[15], characters jump out of their cars to sing and dance in freeway traffic, but such behavior is highly unlikely in a dark, brooding sci-fi, like *Blade Runner*.[16] There are exceptions, of course (see *The Singing Detective*.[17])

In a comic fantasy like *Barbie*[18], how her car operates is not worth much attention, but in a car racing action picture like *Ford vs. Ferrari*[19], how the engines work, and look and sound, gets plenty of loving detail. The cars become characters!

In a silent comedy, if a Little Tramp slips on a banana peel, we laugh, but in a legal thriller it means we are in for a nasty

---

[15] *Lala Land* (2016) Screenplay: Damien Chazelle. Director: Damien Chazelle. Editor: Tom Cross.

[16] *Blade Runner* (1982) Screenplay: Hampton Fancher and David Webb Peoples. Director: Ridley Scott. Editors: Marsha Nakashima and Terry Rawlings.

[17] *The Singing Detective* (2003) Screenplay: Dennis Potter. Director: Keith Gordon. Editor: Jeff Wishengrad.

[18] *Barbie* (2023) Screenplay: Greta Gerwig and Noah Baumbach. Director: Greta Gerwig. Editor: Nick Houy.

[19] *Ford vs. Ferrari* (2019) Screenplay: Jez Butterworth, John-Henry Butterworth, and Jason Keller. Director: James Mangold. Editors: Andrew Buckland, Michael McCusker, and Dirk Westervelt.

lawsuit. So, keep in mind the type of story you're telling, and the genre . . .

"'Cause if you wanna do something out here, it better be one of the five major food groups, or your superiors go napsy-bye."
—David Mamet, *Speed-the-Plow*

Mamet is an American playwright and screenwriter with a deliciously twisted view of the movie business. Look him up.

Sorry. Did my jaded Hollywood cynical alter-ego almost slip out here?

4

Heroes, Villains, and Dubious Characters

A conversation with the audience is underway. Your story has a clear theme, and you know the genre that will guide your choices. All we need is someone to give this story a swift kick in the butt to get it moving. Anybody? Hello? We're losing the light, any volunteers?

We arrive at the point where someone must take up space in the middle of your story. Whose eyes are we looking through? What brave soul (our protagonist) is going to slay the dragon and win the day? In short, whose story, is it? And why should we care about them? Who will anchor you and hold your hand as events unfold? Who will you care about? Will you care about this person?

The main character, who the story is about, is your hero. And how the hero embodies the theme of the story is what builds a bond with the audience. What does this hero care about? What attracts their focus? Do they have character traits (and flaws) that we recognize from our own experience with people in the world?

Classically, the hero is a human descended from the gods who goes on a mission of consequence for a cause greater than themselves. Someone is rescued, the mortal enemy is defeated, the precious elixir/object is recovered and brought back for the People to make their lives whole again. This uber-story is something we've been telling ourselves for a long, long time. But the power of the hero story is very much alive today. Peter Parker, Catniss Everdeen and Homer Simpson are all, in their own way on a hero's quest.

> "The latest incarnation of Oedipus, the continued romance of Beauty and the Beast, stands this afternoon on the corner of 42nd Street and Fifth Avenue, waiting for the light to change."
> —Joseph Campbell,
> *The Hero with a Thousand Faces*

Not only can you find a hero in everyday contemporary life; you can see the hero looking back at you from the mirror. Let's put a pin in that and we'll circle back a little further in Reel 4.

The hero embodies your theme and has recognizable traits that are both positive and negative. Unfortunately, the hero has something essential missing and must go on a kind of adventure or quest to uncover that piece and return to make everyone happy in time for the ending. Michael Moore in *Roger & Me*[20], Diana Nyad in *Nyad*[21] and even, Papi, the little dog in *Beverly Hills Chihuahua*[22], are all heroes on a quest.

ACTING AND EMPATHY

So, the hero goes on a quest. Big deal. What does that have to do with me? Why should I care about them?

Too often, the character we are asked to spend time with is not someone we are likely to hang out with in real life. One way to answer the "Why should I care?" question is to see what the hero cares about so they can model that empathy for us.

Maybe that's why so many heroes have pets. If we see Rocky, the boxer, treat his pet turtles with care, we are persuaded to see him, and so Adrian, his girlfriend, can see him as a caring person, despite his brutish occupation. This makes it feel more natural to care about what happens to him. Sylvester Stallone, for those of you who have been sleeping under a rock, played Rocky.

This ability to create empathy is something that comes mostly from the mysterious craft of acting. The actors create with their physical presence, with their voice along with their

---

[20] *Roger & Me* (1989) Screenplay: Michael Moore. Director: Michael Moore. Editors: Jennifer Bemon and Wendy Stanzler.

[21] *Nyad* (2023) Screenplay: Diana Nyad and Julia Cox. Directors: Jimmy Chin and Elisabeth Chai Vasarhelyi. Editor: Christopher Tellefson.

[22] *Beverly Hills Chihuahua* (2008) Screenplay: Analisa LaBianco and Jeffrey Bushnell. Director: Raja Gosnell. Editor: Sabrina Plisco.

heart and soul to bring their character to life. As an editor, you want to support that vulnerable work by choosing the best of their performances and arrange the pieces in the best possible order. You can help or harm an actor's performance with the timing of how the scenes are put together. This takes sensitivity and emotional awareness to bring out their best performance and make it shine.

A few questions come to mind:

When will a pause convey unspoken depths of feeling? When would it become indulgent and too long?

When is it more interesting to see the listener rather than the actor delivering lines?

Cutting on tiny shifts of eye movement encourages viewers to give their attention to these subtle cues. A lot goes into these choices, and you will refine your own tastes and preferences as you go along.

One method for getting the most out of the performances is to think the way actors do. Ask yourself what the character wants (*objective*) what do they do (*action*) and what's stopping them from getting it (*obstacle*). Then, if they don't succeed, how do they proceed to make a pivot (*adjustment*) and try again in a new direction?

Think about who supports the main character and wants them to win. Who is aligned against the hero and wants them to fail? That's your antagonist—the villain. The dynamic of how these characters relate to each other breathes life into the drama and engages our interest.

PRO TIP

Take an acting class!
At the very least,
learn the vocabulary of actors and directors.
Write a five-minute screenplay with *you* as the star.

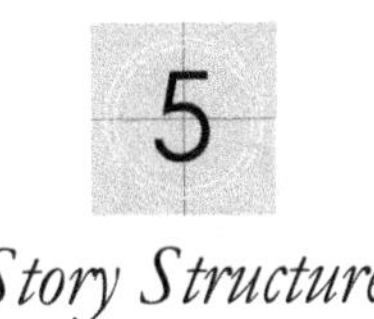

5

Story Structure

Once the story starts to move, the three-act structure has become a flexible template for engaging an audience with a limited attention span. This classic shape is adapted from Aristotle and Greek drama to evolve through the work of Joseph Campbell, Christopher Vogler, and others in the moviemaking era. Despite its flaws, this structure remains a sturdy base for holding attention in all kinds of long-form storytelling. With tongue in cheek, it goes something like this:

ACT ONE

Once upon time, minding her own business, young Polly is suddenly thrown off her perch *(inciting incident)* and from that day forth, nothing would be the same. Polly realizes that what she wants more than anything is a cracker, and she needs to undertake a quest to find one. *(call to adventure)*.

ACT TWO

After some trepidation, she sets off. Enduring several trials and dangers, she reaches a threshold where she can no longer go back home *(point of no return)* and she must embrace her quest, come what may *(decisive moment)*. Without knowing if she will succeed or fail, she takes a bold step forward *(leap of faith)*, only to find her mission is in danger of complete and utter failure. *(all seems lost)*

ACT THREE

Exhausted and alone, the inkling of an idea dawns on her *(glimmer of hope)*, and with newfound determination, she charges into a big fight with the "thing" that scared her the most *(final battle)*. After losing a few feathers, Polly emerges victorious and finds her way home with the cracker of her hard-earned wisdom *(return of the hero)*.

Whether you want to write screenplays yourself or just want to speak clearly in a language writers and producers understand, familiarize yourself with this format for thinking about story. Then, adapt as needed for the story you want to tell.

PRO TIP

Take a screenwriting class!

YOUR HERO

Now, let's look at your hero. Wait, what are you wearing? You're leaving the house dressed like that? A choice must be made. Pinstriped suit or shorts and a T-shirt? A little black dress or warrior armor? With the first decision, multiple choices arise to define what kind of hero you have, what they look like, what they wear and the quirks of their personality. You don't need all the questions answered immediately, but the more details you can share, the easier it will be to persuade an audience to come along for the ride.

Let's not forget that costume designers are storytellers, too. As the brilliant Ann Roth said, "the important thing for the actor to know is that you are there to help them find a character. You're there for them. You're not there for yourself. They're not walking around with a board that says this dress came from Ann Roth. You help the actor find the character. That's all."

So, now our story is ready to go. Our hero has chosen a direction and is moving toward a goal. The audience starts to anticipate the looming challenges ahead and our emotional investment starts to grow. As a storyteller, how can you sustain that feeling of connection from the start all the way to the finish?

Help comes in the form of craft. As an editor and a visual storyteller, you will pick up tools that sustain you and the audience for the rocky journey ahead.

REEL 1
Outtakes

1. The audience is engaged from the very first moment.

2. There's always an unspoken contract with the audience, exchanging their attention for some benefit in entertainment, emotion, and insight.

3. When we watch a drama unfold through time, we carry on an inner dialogue with what's happening.

4. A good story engages the emotions and makes us feel something.

5. To think like an editor, identify and embrace the theme so that all decisions flow from a natural, unifying source.

6. A theme remains static until it is illuminated through the clash of opposites. When that happens, you have drama. Then the story starts to move.

7. *Genre* is how you can add spice to the conversation about what kind of story you're telling and what kind of world we are entering.

8. Each genre has a different set of expectations for how the story unfolds, how people behave within the rules for how that world operates.

9. The ability to create empathy comes mostly from the mysterious craft of acting.

Once you start to realize that a film is the sum of its editing, then editing is the thing you're always looking at.
—*Anthony Minghella*

REEL 2
Learning Your Craft

Learning Your Craft

Hang on, not so fast. I know you're eager to get this show on the road, but before striding off into the unknown, we must acknowledge a critical point. Namely, where are we headed? A hero just can't wander off, swiping through his phone for a map. This decision, where the hero takes the fateful first step, is a *choice*. Some might call it the art of creative discrimination, or in some cases, amputation.

Here's how it works. To get the action moving, the storyteller must choose.

This direction, not *that*.

What's *in* and what's *out*.

Taking that first step is a chance to wield an extremely handy tool.

6

Tools (and Tricks) of the Trade

TOOL #1
THE SWORD OF DISCRIMINATION[23]

When we use the word *discrimination,* let's be clear. We live in sensitive times when our choice of words can land us in hot water or a cold shower. We are talking about discriminating *between* things, not discriminating *against* anyone. Not to "exclude from," but to "recognize a difference." For example, a chef must have a discriminating palette. A music critic takes pride in having a discriminating ear.

To discriminate in this sense is to recognize quality and to make a judgement about suitability. As a creative artist, you discriminate when you decide where a story begins and who initiates the action. By making this initial choice, you begin to

---

[23] Imagine letters rumbling across the screen and lots of reverb on the soundtrack.

define what belongs in the story and what does not. Some elements will naturally fall into place and others will fall by the wayside.

Start by discriminating with the ending. If you know where the climax of the story is headed, why not give us a distance to cover so it makes for a more satisfying journey when we arrive? If we wind up at an artisanal wedding with barefoot bridesmaids in handmade dresses, see if you can start on a crowded underground train at rush hour. If your hero ends up leading a triumphant parade up Fifth Avenue, start with a meek country bumpkin who can't get the tractor started.

Slash away at things that don't belong. Cut out the extraneous and the superfluous so that the stuff that *does* belong will start to shine. Remarkably, once you begin this sword stuff, you quickly become an Edward Scissorhands, snipping, and chopping until you arrive at a pleasing finished shape where all the pieces fit together.

You might start out with a machete to chop through the thick jungle of footage you are working with, and then switch to a scalpel later for fine cutting. It's all part of an ongoing process to sift out the gold and make the best pieces shine.

Throughout this process, you keep an eye on the audience experience to recognize when you have said enough, which calls to mind a fundamental concept when it comes to storytelling, one that has served me well over years of telling stories for the screen.

PRO TIP

Half as long is twice as good.

THE VALUE OF BREVITY

An important aspect of discrimination is considering how long it takes to tell your story. The attention span of any audience is limited, and there are endless options for distraction by pinging phones, screaming children and other stories competing for attention. You want to respect the time your audience is giving you by offering the most streamlined version of what you have to say. Can you make it shorter? See if you can run the scene at double speed. Is anything lost by making it all go by faster? It depends on the particulars, but compressing the action often gives the story a brighter, livelier feel, which can make the original timing look labored and dull. This technique doesn't always work, but you might surprise yourself by letting go of the original tempo and see how quickly you can move things along.

PRO TIP

Feature the good stuff and hide the rest.[24]

IT'S A PROCESS!

"Feature the good stuff and hide the rest."

This motto bears repeating, and I have it written in fire across my "editorial" forehead. It best applies to the first

---

[24] This motto reminds me of eating the mashed potatoes and hiding the peas.

rough draft of a new project, which is often a vulnerable time for the creative team.

The first time seeing your baby up on its feet, there are bound to be some wobbly scenes not yet fully realized. That's the point! Your story is not finished. There's great value in seeing all the elements in context, despite any rough spots, but it can be agonizing to let your colleagues see something that definitely needs more development.

As a film editor, it is good practice to accent the positive, to give your colleagues encouragement to face the glaring flaws that still need to be addressed.

One aspect of discrimination is to recognize what you have that already works well. Identify the elements that give the first glimmer of what this exciting story was meant to be and then figure out how to build from there.

If you have a section of the story that drags, can it be compressed? Eliminated? Do we really need that long talky section where all the characters explain where they were born and went to school?

Feature the elements that are entertaining and minimize the bits that are dull. Simple to say, but tricky to execute. Everyone, but especially the future audience, will be grateful and you'll be relieved to know your instincts were right.

PRO TIP

Rule #1: Don't be boring!

Rule #2: Don't be boring!

Rule #3: Don't be boring!

TOOL #2

TO SHARPEN WITH CONTRAST

Once you choose what's in and what's out, your next mission is to arrange the pieces. Your secret weapon, and a prime principle of visual storytelling, is to convey information through *contrast*.

The classic example is called the Kulashov Effect, where a single closeup of a man's face was intercut together with a shot of a baby in a casket, then a bowl of hot soup, and then a woman lying on a couch. These corresponding shots conveyed sadness, hunger, and lust.

FYI: Lev Kuleshov was a Russian filmmaker who directed his first film in 1917 and taught early Soviet film courses at the National Film School. He wanted to create a distinction between artistic mediums, including cinema, literature, theater, and photography. He was fascinated by the power film editors had to manipulate the emotions of the audience. He posed a discriminating question as part of his studies on film theory. "What differentiates cinema from other mediums?" He believed the answer could be found in how the materials presented were organized. That's how the Kuleshov Effect (also known as the Kuleshov Experiment) was born and continues to influence modern filmmaking more than a century later.

EXPERIMENT

Remember what we said about patterns? Human minds have managed to survive perilous situations for thousands of years by recognizing patterns. It is almost impossible to avoid constructing a pattern from this series of images. So, we see…

Closeup: Man's face (neutral) looking off screen.
Insert: Toddler in a casket.
Closeup: Man's face (neutral) looking off screen.

We look at the man's face and see him "react" to the toddler in a casket. Is this his child? Does he feel grief-stricken for the little one? The poor father!

Closeup: Man's face (neutral) looking off screen.
Insert: Bowl of soup.
Closeup: Man's face (neutral) looking off screen.

Does the man now seem focused on his rumbling belly?

Closeup: Man's face (neutral) looking off screen.
Insert: Woman lying on couch.
Closeup: Man's face (neutral) looking off screen.

Is he now distracted from a devastating loss by feelings of lust? What a cad!

TO CREATE CONVERSATION
THROUGH CONTRAST

By simply contrasting images against each other, the audience pieces together a story, and we launch into a conversation. And you, as a clever storyteller, can apply the right tools to guide this conversation in service of your story.

To illustrate this point while teaching at the London Film School and Emerson College, I asked my students how they would represent a character who is lonely. The most common response suggested a small figure in a big empty space, saying they are "all alone."

Okay, but can't you bring more insight into the emotional life of the character by being more specific and by adding contrast? A small figure in a large space provides us with only the most basic information. What would build a stronger emotional connection between your story and the audience?

What if your character sits alone on a park bench and we notice that she's across from a playground? If she's watching a row of happy parents pushing their toddlers on a swing set, we might get the idea that she's lonely and yearns for a child. We start to give her a story because we see her, notice what she sees, and interpret how she "responds." The audience fills in the blanks based on their own life experience.

Or, if a man looks in through a window at an elegant party where waltzing couples make merry and drink champagne, that creates a more specific flavor to his loneliness, different from a teenager stuck in the middle of a chattering school dance, with her eyes on the window where lacy snowflakes are falling outside.

By showing an individual in relation to others we can recognize what the character lacks and what they yearn for in their life. We learn something about them without having to hear it spoken out loud. The audience has been *invited* to see them as missing something because that's where their attention is focused. A conversation is taking place, and the audience is seduced to find out what happens next . . . and to follow along.

Another challenge I gave my film students was how to present a character who is in a position of royalty, for example, as a king or queen. Here, the lesson is not to show how a single character relates to a group, but rather how the group relates to them.

For example, if a woman sits alone in a chair, we can only glean so much information about her position. She might just be tired of standing and her feet hurt. But once we see a group of people surround her who bow their heads and lower themselves on one knee, her status immediately becomes elevated and she assumes a position of power, like a queen.

Storytelling through contrast can be applied in many ways. You can contrast how differently two characters behave (Walter Matthau as a slob and Jack Lemmon as a neat freak in *The Odd Couple*[25]) or how the music contrasts with the image (Beethoven's Ninth symphony in *A Clockwork Orange*[26]) or how a character changes over time (Scrooge in *A Christmas Carol*[27]). Storytelling through contrast is a rich source of invention that can bring depth to your characters and a rich emotional dimension to your story.

For those of you just beginning to pave your way, how about an example? One of the most powerful uses of visual contrast is in Akira Kurosawa's brilliant film, *IKIRU*[28] *("To Live")*. A government functionary working in a large office receives a diagnosis of stomach cancer. The film opens with a full screen image of his ominous looking x-ray. He goes out with a colleague to a tea shop to share the sad news. As he's talking, we see in the background a group of giddy teenage girls, celebrating a birthday party. They have little hats and balloons and are enjoying a happy, carefree occasion. This contrast makes his story even sadder, doesn't it? If the main

---

[25] *The Odd Couple* (1968). Screenplay: Neil Simon. Director: Gene Saks. Editor: Frank Bracht.

[26] *A Clockwork Orange* (1971). Screenplay: Stanley Kubrick. Director: Stanley Kubrick. Editor: Bill Butler.

[27] *A Christmas Carol,* (2009). Screenplay: Robert Zemeckis. Director: Robert Zemeckis. Editor: Jeremiah O'Driscoll

[28] *IKIRU* (1952). Screenplay: Akira Kurosawa. Director: Akira Kurosawa. Editor: Koishi Iwashita.

character was in a neutral place, the news would be serious but not as emotional. It touches us deeply because we see the joy of life he will be missing. With a subtle visual contrast, we feel this devastating news *with* him. The whole movie is a masterpiece and well worth your time.

Storytelling through contrast gets to the essence of drama. Two opposing forces clash, like order and chaos or freedom and slavery, and we follow the story to find out which side comes out on top. Once we invest in the characters, we go on an emotional journey that lingers in the heart long after the story is finished.

How do you deliver that satisfying result? We have more tools on our belt. Contrast and discrimination are great and always necessary, but it's time to bring out the big guns.

TOOL #3
THE ENGINE OF CAUSE AND EFFECT

This tool becomes the engine to drive your story. While discrimination and contrast get you part way there, cause and effect will generate momentum, creating one moment that leads to another. If the audience leans forward to find out what happens next, then your use of cause and effect is doing its job.

When listening to a story, do you ever notice a moment when you start to get restless? Often, it's because the thread of what's happening no longer builds momentum. The story begins to feel random. One thing happens, then another thing happens, but they don't seem to be related, and the conversation with your audience deflates, like the bubbles in flat champagne.

It's like you have run out of things to say and are desperately clutching at straws to keep things moving. The cure for this awful disease (See Rule #1, 2, 3: Don't be boring!) is to give the events a chain of logic—*this* happens so then *that* happens.

One action *causes* another action. Something happens that triggers a chain reaction of events that ties the story together. This logic can be subtle or obvious, depending on your taste and the specific story you're telling, but every story, from a perfume ad to *The Odyssey*[29], needs something to drive our interest forward.

In *Chicken Run*, which I edited, Rocky, the fast-talking rooster, feels guilty because the hens have put their faith in him, and he knows he can't deliver. Even crusty old Fowler believes him and apologizes by offering his war medal to Rocky. Because he receives the medal (*cause*), Rocky goes up to the rooftop to think things over (*effect*). Up on the roof, he runs into Ginger (*cause*), who softens toward him for the first time (*effect*). Rocky tries to explain himself (*cause*), but her trusting eyes get him all tongue tied (*effect*), and so on.

The chain of events feed off one another and invite us to follow the emotional thread of what's happening between the two characters onscreen. We identify with them because we can follow how they are feeling, moment by moment, and the contours of their relationship to one another. Pretty good acting from these two lumps of modeling clay!

---

[29] One of two major ancient Greek poems attributed to Homer.

In *Frankenweenie*, Victor is heartbroken that his loyal dog, Sparky, is dead (*cause*). He gets the idea to bring Sparky back to life (*effect*), and he secretly gathers the equipment he needs (*cause*) to build an impressive re-animation machine (*effect*).

On a stormy night, Victor puts the dog's body on the machine and hoists it up through the roof (*cause*), where it can be struck by lightning and re-animate (*effect*). He lowers the body to see if the experiment worked (*cause*), but Victor cannot hear a heartbeat (*effect*). He sheds a tear that lands on Sparky (*cause*), and finally, the dog is miraculously alive once again (*effect*)!

This lengthy action scene plays without dialogue to explain what's happening because the audience can easily follow the visual chain of events through *cause and effect*. The conversation takes place visually, and the story is propelled forward by the relationship between images.

When that chain is broken, or in some cases never begun, the audience is left with a feeling of flatness, and the story starts to feel episodic with nothing compelling to drive the story forward. Whatever does happen takes on a random, aimless quality.

You could argue that the random, aimless quality of life is the subject of your story, and for a couple minutes I could believe you. But then think of how you will hold your audience's attention. Do you really want to hear that awful sound of people shifting in their seats, glancing at their watches, and scanning for the nearest exit? I hope you never have to hear it, but if you do, next time you will wish you embraced the powerful tool of *cause and effect*.

As Ralph Waldo Emerson, a 19th century author and scholar, once said, "Shallow men believe in luck. Strong men believe in cause and effect." Ahead of his time, old Waldo would have been a great film editor.

TOOL #4
THE WAVE OF JO-HA-KYU

Time, since you mentioned it, is another key factor in storytelling. It determines how much real time passes by on the clock *and* the perceived time of how long a story takes to play out. Learning to deftly handle time is your next great tool.

Let's consider the Japanese stage for this one and the way they shape a story. *Jo-Ha-Kyu* is a universal element of storytelling that offers a clear, simple way to shape the stories you tell. It goes by many names in different cultures, but translates roughly as beginning, middle and end, or in some contexts, "beginning, break, rapid," which means that all actions or efforts should begin slowly, speed up, and then end swiftly.

Jo: to initiate a movement.

Ha: the rising action.

Kyu: the turning point.

All movement can be described as having *Jo-Ha-Kyu*—everything from a single breath to an entire lifetime. Think of a wave breaking on the shore. Its natural action starts in a clear direction, then momentum builds as the wave gathers force, and it finally reaches an energetic peak as it crashes on the beach. Afterward, there's a moment of calm that leads into a new direction and the cycle continues.

Each individual scene has *Jo-Ha-Kyu,* and your overall story can be considered this way. You might consider it to have good *Jo,* or an overlong *Ha,* or if the story has been built well, a satisfying *Kyu.*

Take a simple movement, such as stamping your foot, which is a common gesture in the Japanese theatre. You raise your foot, with *Jo,* from stillness to movement. With *Ha,* the foot speeds up as it moves down to strike the floor. Then with *Kyu,* the foot lands with a thump and returns to stillness.

JO-HA-KYU AND ANIMATION

This concept has given me a guiding principle when facing the challenges of animation editing. An animated movie is not produced like a live action movie. In live action, everyone gets the script; the movie is shot based on the script, and then the shots are cut together by the editor. In animation, the production team needs more detail than what can be found in the words alone, so storyboards are drawn to create a comic book version of the movie.

The editor's task is to make these simple sketches look like moving images. Then, by adding dialog and sound, the creative team can watch the entire movie in storyboard form. Decisions can be made about pacing and story before committing to the expensive process of animating every frame.

So, how do you make stills look like they're moving? Applying Jo-Ha-Kyu is the best way I found to create little peaks of energy. By adjusting the time for each sketch gives the illusion of movement and carries the viewer along.

Everything from a single character's expression to the entire story will benefit from this gathering sense of rhythm.

Jo-Ha-Kyu is the secret password to better storytelling.

Every individual scene can be said to express *Jo-Ha-Kyu*. It doesn't matter if two characters are building up to a first kiss or a punch in the nose. It feels most natural if the action slowly builds with a quickening pace until it reaches a peak moment, like the crescendo in musical terms. After a pause, the story continues. Because this shape of movement is so natural, audiences will be swept along by the story because the rhythm feels right. If you've ever taken a music appreciation class, you might remember that a sonata has three parts: exposition, development, and recapitulation. This is similar to a series of film scenes, flowing one into another, engaging the audience with a dynamism that propels the story forward.

For example, early in *The Tale of Despereaux,* a terrine of soup is being presented at an elaborate banquet, while up in the rafters, a rat scurries along, drawn by the delicious smell. The tension builds as the soup and the rat draw closer together, and the pace quickens, until at last, just as the King lifts the spoon to his lips, the rat tumbles down and falls with a splash. The tension is finally released, and we achieve a (hopefully) comic effect.

Many so-called "experts" drone on and on about stories needing a beginning, middle and end. But just because a story starts somewhere and goes someplace else, it doesn't mean it won't get boring. It's not enough to follow the steps laid out if they all come in the same size and shape and fall into the same plodding rhythm. I've heard it called "hook, build up and payoff," which sounds more like a proposition delivered while leaning into a car window.

Jo-Ha-Kyu provides a refined tool that offers a more dynamic approach. You can build a story that makes the best use of natural rhythms and your audience's attention.

Jo-Ha-Kyu goes hand in hand with the other tools, like *cause and effect.* If the action has the internal logic of a chain of events and the natural rhythm of Jo-Ha-Kyu, you can carry (and keep) the viewers' attention over a longer period.

TOOL #5

THE SUPER POWER OF BENDING TIME

This tool is an expansion of Jo-Ha-Kyu. Not only can you subtly change time by building scenes in a natural rhythm; you can stretch and bend time to suit your needs.

Let's consider your story visually as a timeline, running across the bottom of your screen, as the minutes and seconds pass by. How you stretch or compress that timeline signals to your viewers what is important and worth their consideration. It's also tipping off what is unnecessary and can be skipped over.

In *2001: A Space Odyssey,*[30] an epic jump cut takes us from a primitive man throwing a bone in the air to a space station majestically orbiting the Earth. We suddenly find ourselves leaping thousands of years into the future, a clear signal that

---

[30] *2001: A Space Odyssey* (1968). Screenplay: Stanley Kubrick, Arthur C. Clarke. Director: Stanley Kubrick. Editor: Ray Lovejoy.

anything that happened between those two events is not worth our attention.

Later in the same movie, when the astronaut Bowman must de-activate the computer HAL, essentially killing him, every moment is stretched and expanded to wring out as much pathos as possible.

Think of a time when something dramatic happened in your own life. Did you have the sensation of time slowing down? At that moment, didn't each of your senses become heightened? Did you become aware of details that you hadn't noticed before? For example, the way your throat felt suddenly dry, or the sensation of your feet on the floor. This effect is re-created in visual stories all the time and is a great tool to become familiar with and use.

As a filmmaker, you can manipulate time. It's your superpower. Use it wisely to give your story a dynamic shape. Compress and expand time to serve the subjective truth of your story.

For example, when I was a young boy, I learned how to play whiffle ball. I had a yellow plastic bat and a white plastic ball, and I tried to hit fungoes. Holding the bat with one hand, I tossed up the ball with the other, then quickly grabbed the bat with both hands to swing at the ball on its way down. Over and over, I missed. With each attempt, I grew more frustrated, and I swung harder and harder. Then it finally happened. Bat met ball and time stopped. I stared at the ball, following its flight as it soared upward as the moment stretched out in silence. It was beautiful until thunk! The ball fell to Earth, and I started my quest all over again.

What's your version? For example, when you tell your friend about what happened yesterday, you might say something like this:

"I woke up and brushed my teeth, same as usual, and when I walked to the kitchen a giant alien grabbed the toaster and ate it all up in one gulp. Then, I put on my jacket, grabbed my keys, and walked out the door."

By giving all these actions the same emphasis (and time), you fail to convey what is extraordinary about your story. For sure, your friend would stop you and say, "Whoa! An alien? In your freaking kitchen? I didn't get that. Go back and tell me again."

Just like your friend, an audience needs time to take in what is unusual and unexpected. We can't go on to "what happens next" if we can't follow what just happened. This is another case of expanding the moments that make your story special and compressing the events that don't merit the attention.

Let's consider the "getting to know you" montage in a romantic comedy. We've seen this many times. A happy couple goes to the movies, walks through the park with ice cream cones, until they finally steal a chaste goodnight kiss at the front door, etc. We know what's happening. They are getting to know each other. Do we need to know the price of the ice cream cones or who paid for what? Unless this story is about the economics of dating, then no, we don't. We can skip over those details and get to the relationship drama of tears and confession that will come up soon because conflict, of course, is the heartbeat of any romantic comedy.

PRO TIP

When there's no conflict, compress the action.
When there's a life-or-death struggle, stretch time.
Sustain the drama and milk it for all it's worth.

LET IT BREATHE!

Another time bending example is a scene from the Tarantino movie, *Pulp Fiction.*[31] Mia (Uma Thurman) has accidentally overdosed and lies on the floor, unconscious. Vincent (John Travolta) is desperate to revive her before her gangster boyfriend finds out. At a friend's apartment, he gets hold of a medical kit with an adrenaline shot that must be plunged directly into her heart.

After a frantic effort to prepare the injection, Vincent fumbles with the instructions, and we hear voices overlapping as he yells for a Sharpie to mark the spot on Mia's chest where the needle will go. Characters crowd into the wide frame, rushing in and out, building a froth of nervous tension as Mia lies there, unmoving. Then, suddenly, once Vincent raises the hypodermic needle above her chest, everything slows down and gets quiet. We see a closeup of the needle, Mia's unconscious face, two onlookers leaning in, Vincent, and then back to the dripping needle. The tension is riveting, and time is stretched out to make the most of it.

This moment exemplifies the power of bending time.

---

[31] *(Pulp Fiction* (1994). Screenplay: Quentin Tarantino. Director: Quentin Tarantino, Editor: Sally Menke.

7

Hana, the Gift That Keeps on Giving

This tool is the jewel, the one all others serve. *Hana* is the Japanese word for "blossom" and represents the highest climactic moment of your story. If the rhythm has been well-constructed, the audience is breathing completely in sync with the performers as the pace gathers intensity and the noise leads to a rare moment of calm, like a parting of the clouds.

In the space after the Kyu, and just before a new Jo begins, there's a moment of stillness with a rare mysterious quality. It's like a tipping point, and it functions as a hinge before the movement begins again. At the highest point of the whole story, the peak moment, the climax, this moment of stillness blossoms into something larger and more beautiful. Like a gift, something is conveyed in that moment, something like a revelation, that will live long in one's memory after the story is finished.

This moment is the reason we bought a ticket and suspended our disbelief to hear this story in the first place. It's a moment of calm after the storm, when a secret is shared that gives us something valuable and true to take home with us.

In *Whale Rider,*[32] a Maori girl has struggled throughout the story to convince her grandfather to choose her to embody the ritual of riding a killer whale. No girl had ever done this before, and he angrily refuses. But with no boys fit for the honor, it finally falls to her and the moment she goes into the sea to take hold of the killer whale's dorsal fin, her ride on its back is quiet and mysterious and opens like a flower.

In *E.T.,*[33] we see it and feel it as the kids desperately pedal their bikes to carry their alien friend to safety, hounded by adults, at risk of capture, injury or worse. At the last moment, their bicycle lifts off the ground and their silhouettes fly across the moon and they land far away in a place of safety. That moment of wonder is *Hana,* a blossoming flower.

In Charlie Chaplin's *City Lights,*[34] when the formerly blind flower girl realizes that the Little Tramp is the one who paid for her eye operation, the moment leaves her thunderstruck and his smile opens like a flower. *Hana.*

Chaplin also famously said, "You'll never find rainbows if you're looking down."

---

[32] *Whale Rider* (2002), Screenplay: Nick Caro and Witi Ihimaera. Director: Niki Caro. Editor: David Coulson.

[33] *ET: The Extra-Terrestrial* (1982). Screenplay: Melissa Mathison. Director: Steven Spielberg. Editor: Carol Littleton.

[34] *City Lights* (1931): Screenplay: Charles Chaplin. Director: Charles Chaplin. Editor: Charles Chaplin.

A true storyteller knows that with this moment of realization, the gift has been delivered.

61

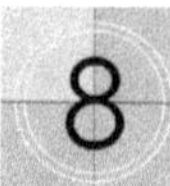

Baloney Cow

You wouldn't think that cattle ranchers have much in common with film editors, but you'd be surprised. Okay, so your saddle is on wheels in a darkened suite of rooms, while cowboys ride under big open skies, but there's something a practiced eye can see that will save you a lot of heartache.

Maybe I should call it Tool #6.

From up on their horse or pickup truck, an experienced rancher will look at a herd of grazing cows and quickly size up the potential value they represent. The best cattle, the prize of the herd, with robust health and a strong frame, if treated right, are destined to become fine steaks. High value.

Then, there's a middle batch of cows that are perfectly fine, just not top of the line, and are best suited to a future as hamburgers.

And then, there's the last batch of cows, the lower rung, where no matter how you cut it, these cattle will only ever be good for baloney.

This reminds me of one of Billy Wilder's prescient quotes: "We are on the track of something absolutely mediocre."

Sometimes, you must face the fact that the movie you're editing, despite your best efforts, will only ever be a baloney cow. You do your best, but that's just the way it is. Drop 15 and punt. Declare victory and move on.

REEL 2
Outtakes

1. To get the action moving, the storyteller must choose. *This* direction, not *that*. What's *in* and what's *out*. Taking that first step is a chance to use an extremely handy tool.

2. To discriminate is to recognize quality and to judge suitability. As a creative artist, you discriminate when you decide where a story begins and who initiates the action.

3. "Half as long is twice as good."

4. "Feature the good stuff and hide the rest."

5. Rule #1: Don't be boring!

6. Your secret weapon is to convey information through *contrast*.

7. Time is a key factor in storytelling. It determines how much real time passes by *and* the perceived time of how long a story takes to play out.

8. Jo-Ha-Kyu is the secret password to better storytelling. It provides a refined tool that makes the best use of natural rhythms and your audience's attention.

9. *Hana*, the Japanese word for "blossom," represents the highest climactic moment of your story. If the rhythm has been well-constructed, the audience is breathing completely in sync with the performers as the pace gathers intensity and the noise leads to a rare moment of calm, like a parting of the clouds.

10. Sometimes, you must face the fact that the movie you're editing, despite your best efforts, will only ever be a baloney cow. You do your best, but that's just the way it is. Drop 15 and punt. Declare victory and move on.

I have ten commandments.
The first nine are, thou shalt not bore.
The tenth is, thou shalt have right of final cut.
—*Billy Wilder*

REEL 3
Embracing the Freelance Life

Embracing the Freelance Life

Telling stories as a film editor involves more than knowing the tools of the trade and how to use them. What you do facing the screen represents only one third of the job. That's right, a *third.*

The rest is about your relationships with people, including yourself. Because the hard truth is this: *what you know about storytelling won't matter if you can't get hired.* Your skills and knowledge need an opportunity to be expressed in the real world on a platform you build for yourself or join up with as a freelancer.

So, let's talk about that. The freelance life of an editor.

We may seem to be right back where we started, on the outside looking in, with a sheer wall to climb. Before showing off your amazing storytelling skills, first you need an opportunity. And without professional credits or warm introductions to open doors, finding a point of entry can be daunting and not everyone succeeds.

It's easy to get lost in the freelance gig economy. Especially today, with the rapid pace of globalization and technological advances, you need to navigate choppy waters. The 2023 strike by writers and actors vividly illustrated the turmoil in the entertainment business.

Where to be? Proximity to the center of the "industry" has value, especially when you are starting out. It demonstrates your commitment to put yourself at the heart of the action. For the entertainment business, that means Los Angeles, where you will meet more people and discover more opportunities than anywhere else in the English-speaking world. Every city has its own culture, and The City of Angels is a world of its own.

So, slip on a pair of Ray-Bans, grab a green smoothie from the drive thru, and go for a ride with the sunroof open. You'll love L.A.

NO PEDIGREE, LOTS OF SELF-CONFIDENCE

When I moved out west to pursue a career in the movie business, I had $300 to my name; I was driving a battered little French sedan with a balky transmission, and I had two local friends in my Rolodex to call. I had no pedigree from a fancy film school and no useful family connections. But I had the self-belief to find my way into a competitive business.

I spent a year living in a studio apartment with no furniture, just a futon and a clock radio for company. Eventually, I gained a foothold as an apprentice film editor and started to work my way up. I was able to sustain a career as a freelance editor and worked with some of the leading lights in Hollywood, people like Mel Gibson, Emily Blunt, and Ivan Reitman. It wasn't the overwhelming success I had dreamt of, but I was able to support my family with a creative role on well-regarded movies, like *Shrek*, *Space Jam*, and *Chicken Run*, movies that general audiences (especially kids) continue to adore.

But in the beginning, it was a lonely hill to climb.

The Goalposts Keep Moving

Starting a freelance career of any kind is daunting. Keeping up with rapid shifts in the landscape can be perplexing and decent gigs are hard to find. Once hired, you feel squeezed by producers who relentlessly focus on the bottom line—driving down costs.

I remember showing up for one gig on a B-movie where the producer refused to pay for meals and gave everyone on the crew an empty lunchbox. Unsurprisingly, morale was flatter than a stale cookie.

You're entering a field where the lifestyle and work hours can be all-consuming. You may find yourself turning down invitations to socialize or attend family celebrations so you can meet a sudden deadline or pitch in as a good team player.

If you're not careful, you can suffer from stress as you fall into unhealthy habits. You must expect to look after yourself and not depend on others to protect you. After all, your health and your work/life balance are your own responsibility. If you join a union that offers some protection, count your blessings. But if you're new or ineligible for membership, you will have to find ways to stay sane, and healthy while you keep that winning smile.

What if the years go by and the promising career isn't keeping its promise? It's easy to get discouraged and give into the temptation to throw your hands up, fall into hopelessness and abandon the idea. Go do something else. Get a real job. It can seem like nobody cares about stories, especially yours.

But stories matter. So, what's an ambitious film editor to do?

Without the necessary savvy, it's hard to see a viable future, because you are still learning what makes a good story tick.

Personally, you may lack the resources to combat stress and a nagging sense of disillusionment. Along the way, you may have lost the enthusiasm and passion that got you started down this road in the first place. You may ask yourself, "How will this ever get better?"

I worked nights in Palm Springs on a low-budget indie production and visited the set where all the extras were covered in guacamole for the big comic finale, looking exhausted and unhappy. They reminded me of a circus hand, hired to clean up after the elephants. When asked why he didn't quit, he replied incredulously, "What, and leave show business?"

But still, stories *do* matter.

Instead of breathlessly chasing after the latest trends on TikTok, or grabbing every crummy gig that comes along, what if it were possible to make durable progress? What if you could feel confident in the value of what you have to offer? What if you could meet and work with real pros on real projects that move people emotionally with unforgettable stories? What if you could secure projects that pay well and treat you with respect?

Here is the question worth asking:

Whose circle do you want to travel in?

An important part of being a freelancer is to cultivate allies and form bonds for mutual benefit. Sharing news and gossip and knowing who can offer a shoulder to lean on, a place to crash, or news of a possible paying gig, are all part of a productive freelance life. They are as necessary as the nuts and bolts of storytelling.

Whether it's with fellow film school alums, or members of online chatrooms, seeking out a community of mutual support is vital. The only drawback is that people whose career is in the same boat as yours may view you as competition.

VOLLEYBALL FOR NEWBIES

During my first summer in Los Angeles, when I was still feeling my way into the city, a friend told me about a generous TV writer who opened her backyard on Tuesday evenings for a game of volleyball. Her name escapes me, but I will always remember her as a good angel who invited people new to Los Angeles to play and socialize in a fun, informal setting. More casual and relaxed than a meetup, she recognized the value of offering freelancers a kindhearted place to gather and make new connections. In a town with so many isolated newcomers arriving daily, she created an oasis of camaraderie and goodwill. I hope that this weekly game, or something like it, is still going strong, providing a weekly dose of optimism for all the young hopefuls who come to Los Angeles.

An alternative way to find helpful allies is to look to older generations, people who have years of experience and aren't competing with you to get a foot in the door. They can become your advisor, ally or even a mentor.

A true supporter will share their wisdom and experience without expecting more than your attention in return. As you navigate the twists and turns of freelance work, finding a mentor can offer a broader perspective and support, even when they don't offer you a direct paying job.

A BARNACLE ON THE GOOD SHIP HOLLYWOOD

After living in my studio apartment for a few months, I realized I was getting nowhere, and even worse, I didn't have a clue how I'd ever get anywhere else. The ways of Hollywood were a mystery to me. I was befuddled by the intricate politics of drive-on passes, validated parking, assistants within assistants who never have time to talk, and an answering service[35] that never answers a call.

I was on the outside looking in, desperate to find my place. I could imagine a future where I was excited to go to work every day with the opportunity to learn from the best in the

---

[35] Before the age of Task Rabbit, and SMS, an *answering service* provided a live person to answer your calls and collect messages. But most often, they just let you know that you're "all clear."

business. Scattering my resume around town like everyone else wasn't going to cut it. I needed to do something different, so I decided to try a more personalized approach and made a list of the movies I most enjoyed and went to the library to research who had been the editors. (This was the early 1990's before clicking through IMDb was an option. How primitive!)

As a freelancer, how you look for work demonstrates how you will do the job. If you have a positive attitude, don't discourage easily, and show a passion for making visual stories come alive, you will surely get noticed.

What I wanted was names. By digging through the Editors Guild handbook and the Moton Picture Industry Almanac, I created a list of about 15 editors and focused on the ones who listed their contact details. I wrote a personalized letter to each one, including titles of their movies I had most admired. I asked to work as their apprentice, and in closing, I offered to pass on what they would teach me to the next generation, a promise I am keeping now by writing this book that you hold in your hands. And this was before "pay it forward" was a thing.

At the time, Carol Littleton was my favorite editor. She had edited *The Big Chill*[36], *ET: The Extra-Terrestrial*, and *The Manchurian Candidate*[37], so I focused on writing my letter to her, which went something like this:

---

[36] *The Big Chill* (1983). Screenplay: Lawrence Kasdan and Barbara Benedek. Director: Lawrence Kasdan. Editor: Carol Littleton.
5 *The Manchurian Candidate* (2004). *Screenplay:* Richard Condon, George Axelrod, Danile Pyne. *Director:* Jonathan Demme. Editor: Carol Littleton.

December 5, 1989

Carol Littleton
Los Angeles, CA

Dear Carol Littleton,

As an aspiring filmmaker, I request the opportunity to serve as your apprentice.

With so many vivid memories of films you have edited, especially *E.T.* and *The Big Chill*, I hold your work in the highest regard, and hope to emulate the standards you have set.

I was struck, in research for this apprenticeship, by your sensitivity and ability to articulate what motivates your editorial decisions. To work as your apprentice would be an honor.

I bring good humor and a heart full of enthusiasm to this challenging position. Five years of theatre experience as a performer and director has sharpened my instinct for uncovering the spine of a story.

And, more recently, I have been fortunate to assist Rob Kobrin and Victor Nord, two fine editors who share a passion for filmmaking and the generosity to teach a curious assistant. But low-budget productions often require accepting results that are less than fully professional. I yearn for the opportunity to work on material worthy of the big screen, and to meet the most exacting standards. I want to find within myself the eyes, the ears, and the hands of a film editor.

And so, in kinship with the long history of young (and not so young) apprentices in all fields of endeavor, I knock at the master's door seeking entry to the secrets of your art. I promise to respect those secrets and to one day return your kindness by passing on what I learn to the next generation.

Thank you and happy holidays.

A week later, I followed up with each editor by phone, and once a month after that, I sent a postcard to their agent or their published address to remind them of my existence and share whatever news I had. I stayed positive, polite, and persistent.

So, what happened? Eventually, after six months, the phone rang and I heard from Antony Gibbs, a brilliant English editor. Tony had edited several amazing films, such as *Walkabout,*[38] *Performance,*[39] and *Jesus Christ Superstar.*[40]

Rollerball[41] was the recent film that had impressed me most, a science fiction movie centered on a violent gladiator arena, like roller derby, starring James Caan. It was fast, inventive, and gripping entertainment, and I knew a lot of that was because of the editor. I wanted to learn from Tony, who was wrapping up work on a location shoot in Mexico and would be returning to L.A., where he would need an extra hand in the cutting room.

I was thrilled beyond belief. This was a union gig, paying decent money, and I was now on my merry, professional way.

It all started from my initial effort of contacting editors and demonstrating the attitude, doggedness, and good manners I would bring to the job.

By the way, I did eventually speak to Carol who was very encouraging, but she had decided to hire female assistants to give women an opportunity to advance in a male-dominated arena. Fair enough.

So, the path to a breakthrough went something like this: Nothing. Nothing. Nothing . . .

Nothing . . . Maybe . . .

---

[38] *Walkabout* (1971). Screenplay: Luc Roeg, David Gulpilil, Edward Bond. Director: Nicolas Roeg. Editor: Antony Gibbs.

[39] *Performance* (1970). Screenplay: Donald Cammell. Directors: Donald Cammell and Nicolas Roeg. Editor: Antony Gibbs.

[40] *Jesus Christ Superstar* (1973). Screenplay: Norman Jewison and Melvyn Bragg. Director: Norman Jewison. Editor: Antony Gibbs.

[41] *Rollerball* (1975). Screenplay: William Harrison. Director: Norman Jewison. Editor: Antony Gibbs.

Nothing.
More nothing.
(Sigh.)
Success!

10

Opportunity Knocks

Once you do schedule a meeting, show your respect and professionalism by scanning for news about the person you are about to meet. Look at their picture. If you know their work, say you're a fan. Be specific. Remember the importance of a firm handshake and making eye contact. If you're not used to it, practice. Accept interviews for jobs you don't necessarily want so you can get used to talking about yourself without all the stress.

Practice being concise, articulate, and good natured, developing skills that will come in handy when something important is on the line.

THE INTERVIEW

Most interviews start with an open question, so be prepared to respond accordingly.

"So, Mr. So-and-So, tell me about yourself."

First, feel your own two feet on the floor, and if you're nervous, resist the urge to rush. Share your story and demonstrate that you know what this line of work is about. Highlight what is unique and memorable about you. Share an anecdote that shows your positive qualities. Pay attention to the surroundings. What movie posters are on the walls? What are people wearing? Do you get a sense of the office culture? Gather clues and mirror your future colleagues to show what a good fit you will be for the position offered. Practice with your friends, so you become familiar with likely scenarios you may face.

NEGOTIATE!

Until you become established with a list of credits on completed projects, you don't have much leverage to negotiate terms. But negotiation is a valuable skill to develop as you pursue a freelance career.

What points of flexibility will make you a happy camper? Beyond the salary, be clear about what makes a difference for you in terms of working hours, travel, parking, perks, and onscreen credits. Eventually, these will all become deal points to negotiate, and they are unlikely to change after you're hired, so it's best to get them in writing upfront. And once you negotiate successfully on one contract, you've set a precedent for future projects.

For example, once I earned a lead editor credit on a few films, I decided that it was meaningful to see my name on the movie poster. Editors on live-action films are frequently included in the 'credit block' on big movie posters in theater lobbies and I thought editors of animated features deserved the same recognition. I hadn't seen any of my colleagues credited like that before, so I considered it a point worth negotiating. Once I was successful, it provided a precedent for my credits on future films. It may seem like a minor thing, but it was important to me at the time. Your interests may differ.

It's important to get the terms right, because most every job has rough patches that range from uncomfortable to excruciating. In fact, a top cinematographer once said, "All movies start with dinners in a nice restaurant, talking about the palette of the film. And by the end, you're just happy to get out of there alive."

So, if things get stuck in the muck, it's good to remember why you took the gig in the first place. Was it for the money? The people? The script? The exotic location? Keep your eye on the prize to get you through the dark days. If nothing else, you'll have a memorable war story to share.

For instance, the first movie I edited in Montreal was for an independent producer with a charming story about a heroic dog in World War I, called *SGT STUBBY: An American Hero*.[42] It was a barebone budget, and I knew a scrappy indie production would have its drawbacks, but when I learned that the composer was going to be Patrick Doyle, I was all in. Patrick had written some gorgeous movie music, and I was especially fond of his work on *Henry V*.[43] I found one piece of

---

[42] *SGT STUBBY: An American Hero* (2018). Screenplay: Richard Lanni and Mike Stokey. Director: Richard Lanni. Editor: Yours Truly.
[43] *Henry V* (1989). Screenplay: William Shakespeare and Kenneth Branagh. Director: Kenneth Branagh. Editor: Michael Bradsell.

music in that score to be always thrilling, which was played under Henry's big speech to the troops on St. Crispin's Day.

It was the single most exciting piece of movie music I had ever heard, and the idea of working together on a movie with that same composer was entirely persuasive. I knew I had to do it.

SEESAW

Once you get your foot in the door with a working credit or two, the next step is figuring out how to advance. A helpful way to think about choosing projects is to picture a seesaw. On one end of the seesaw is your role and the credit you will earn, and on the other end is the scale and profile of the project.

For example, in the beginning, you are most likely to get an entry level or apprentice position on a smaller project. Then, once you have that experience, you can qualify for the same position on a bigger project, or you can focus on getting a more significant role, such as assistant editor on the same scale show.

Once you prove yourself with a bigger role and more responsibility, you can move up from assistant to associate editor, which is a more creative role. Back and forth on the seesaw you go, building relationships and earning credits as you grow your career.

Other freelance film careers work in a similar way. Camera, production design, costume, and other creative freelancers all face similar challenges.

If you feel stuck on the same kind of picture, or feel restless with the same kind of role, think of the seesaw as giving you a strategy to move ahead as you earn trust and a good reputation in the business. With patience, you can build a solid foundation so you can seize opportunities when they arise.

INSIDE JOB

Once you're hired, become a valuable crew member. Understand the lines of communication. Who in the production office is your best point of contact? Which departments will you be working with most? Who's the head of each department? When you're part of a crew, it's like a military campaign. A chain of command will be assigned different responsibilities, and it's a good idea to be familiar with who's who and how you are expected to fit in.

On a bigger picture, the staff of an editing department can be as large as 20 or more. This consists of an apprentice or two who field calls and emails, a coordinator who goes to production meetings and manages the calendar, someone to take notes at working sessions, assistants to manage all the picture and sound coming in and out of the department, someone to liaise with the marketing and publicity departments, those who deal with visual and special effects, and a couple of associate editors working on scenes to support the lead editor, who works closely with the director and producers to deliver the final cut.

On a smaller scale production, a lot of these roles are combined, and a one-person department is not unheard of on a shoestring budget. Every project has its own demands and limitations in terms of making the best use of available resources.

CHECK YOUR 'TUDE

Your most important allegiance is to the department you're in. If you're with editing, that's your platoon, and the Editor is the Head of Department (HoD). Your department is your priority. The same is true if you're with costume, camera, art, or transportation. You want to be an asset to your department and do what needs to be done. If you focus on solving problems instead of complaining about your job, you are much more likely to be well-remembered and rehired.

Your attitude counts. Schedules can be grueling, and everyone will grow tired and irritable at some point. If you can maintain a sunny professional attitude, especially in California, you contribute to the overall wellbeing of the crew and ultimately do yourself a favor.

DRESS SMART

Pay attention to what you wear. This may seem insignificant, as film crews wear casual, comfortable clothes, but if you're dressed like a child, you're less likely to be treated as an adult. Notice what clothes people wear and how it affects their authority in relation to other crew members. Be comfortable but be clean.

COMMUNICATE!

Contribute to a high standard of creative excellence. Deliver on what is asked of you. If there will be an unavoidable delay, say so. If you can't find a solution, ask for help.

Remember: the obstacles you face, and how they make you feel, are less interesting than you overcoming them and getting the job done.

WOULD YOU CRAWL THROUGH BROKEN GLASS?

On my first day of a new job, I showed up early, ready to make myself useful. I got into the building, but the door to the production office was locked. No one was around, but I was determined to be inside and get acquainted with my new surroundings. It had been a real challenge to get this job, and I wanted to make the most of it.

After a few minutes of pacing, waiting for someone with a key to show up, I noticed a transom above the office door that was open for ventilation. The glass had been smashed, but it looked like a possible entry point, so I stacked some boxes on a chair and climbed up for a closer look. I brushed aside some glass pieces and pulled myself through the passage to safely drop down inside.

I heard footsteps in the hall, so I opened the door and saw the producer standing there with her key. She pieced together what must have happened and looked at me strangely.

"So, wait, you crawled through broken glass to get inside to work?"

I admitted that was the case, not sure how she would react. Maybe this wasn't such a great idea and a reckless insurance risk. She smiled.

"I like it. You're going to get along just fine here."

Believe me, I remembered that!

I don't suggest bleeding out, but persistence pays.

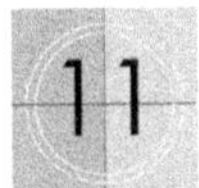

The Power of No and Yes

After assisting Tony on three different films, I felt ready to move up and start cutting films myself. I wanted to get my hands on a project that would give me a chance to make decisions with real footage and try out my ideas about putting a story together.

Without pay, I cut a University of Southern California student short and a documentary film that didn't go anywhere. I felt compelled to find a new opportunity anyway I could.

I realized that one of the most important ways to manage a freelance career is to be choosy. Every year, lots of movies get made in Los Angeles, and many of them are dreadful. Someone makes them, though, and they offer paying work when you don't have many options. But be careful. Working with dodgy producers on mediocre material can get discouraging. And if that's all your work history shows, it becomes a tricky box to escape.

That's not why I came to L.A. Didn't I want to work with top professionals on worthwhile projects I could feel good about? I wanted to form good relations with top creatives and feel proud of the work I was sending out to a global audience. How about you?

THE POWER OF 'NO'

One of the powers you have as a freelancer is the power to say "No" to projects you don't want to be associated with—under any circumstances. Whatever the reason—content, people, or job title—you can choose to say no, thank you, and you'll get less offers along those lines.

On reflection, what mattered to me most was content. I decided to make a boundary and understand that some projects would be better off without me.

I did not want to work on porn.

I did not want to work on horror movies.

Saying "No" helped to define what I wanted to say "Yes" to, i.e., what I really wanted. Other editors feel differently, but I knew that working on porn or horror movies would make me unhappy, which meant I also would not do my best work.

When a producer called to see if I would cut *Children of the Corn 4*, I said "No, thanks."

When a guy with an Australian accent called with an offer to cut something hardcore, I politely said "No" before hanging up as quickly as possible.

As you establish yourself in a freelance career, the credits you earn become the lens for how people see you. If you have four credits on underwater thrillers, you are more likely to get a call for the next *Aquaman* sequel. But if your heart's desire is to work on a Victorian era costume drama, you need to demonstrate some experience with the style. When you want to escape a sub-genre, make sure to pursue projects that build your credits in a different direction. It may take some time, but you'll be happier in the long run.

For example, I didn't expect to have a long list of credits editing animated features, but that's what my choices built. How did that happen?

THE POWER OF 'YES'

When I first said "Yes" to animation, the opportunity was for a couple of weeks of work at Hanna-Barbera (HB). I knew the studio's name from cartoons I loved as a kid.

The Flintstones, The Jetsons and *Scooby Doo* were like mother's milk, and it sounded like great fun to spend a few weeks at the studio, helping to update their editing systems and get the staff comfortable with some new digital tools.

I was looking for a place with equipment to cut a documentary film I had shot about a medical trek in Nepal. If I could work at the cartoon studio during the day (not porn and not horror) and use their editing system after hours to complete my Nepal project, it would be a win-win situation.

A couple weeks of work turned into a few months, which is not unusual in freelance work. If your skillset and demeanor are a good fit for a workplace, people will find reasons to keep you around. Hanna-Barbera, like the rest of Hollywood, was in the throes of a wrenching transition from analog to digital filmmaking and figuring out how to update the sprocket-driven process with new computer-based tools. It was a compelling puzzle to work on.

As a wonderful bonus, I got to hear stories from the Hanna-Barbera sound people who created all those amazing original sound effects. The stories of how the effects were created and how they were named, including the difference between a *skid,* a *bent skid,* and a *broken skid,* were a fascinating slice of film history I heard first-hand from craftspeople like Pat Foley, who created them.

I knew that Disney had been having success with animated movies, like *Little Mermaid*[44] and *The Lion King*[45], but I never considered this corner of moviemaking to be something for me. HB was just a temporary gig until I could finish my documentary.

Then one fine day, my name was volunteered to assist over at Warner Brothers. They were starting up a top-secret project that would be just a few weeks of work to figure out how best to use new digital tools. I was curious enough to say "Yes."

This project turned out to be *Space Jam,* the basketball movie starring Michael Jordan and Bugs Bunny, and it changed the direction of my entire career. I was working on a big studio feature as an Associate Editor with lots of resources

---

[44] *Little Mermaid* (1989) Screenplay: Ron Clements and John Musker. Directors: Ron Clements and John Musker. Editor: Mark A. Hester.

[45] *The Lion King* (1994) Screenplay: Irene Mecchi, Jonathan Roberts, and Linda Woolverton. Directors: Roger Allers and Rob Minkoff. Editor: Ivan Bilancio.

and plenty of pressure to solve problems on the fly to meet a tight deadline.

The scale was bigger than anything I had experienced, and it was exciting to know this project had the potential to become a pop culture touchstone for basketball fans, Looney Tunes fans and moviegoers in general. This was a major studio production with big expectations and a huge effort required to get it all done. Michael Jordan was an international icon! Maybe even bigger than Bugs.

The work reminded me of collaborating in the theatre and felt familiar. Many of the crew members were also from a theatre background, and over several months we became a tight knit creative team.

Without planning to, I had become part of a wave of people who knew their way around an animated feature film. I had proved myself in the heat of a high-stress assignment and knew that I wanted to work with these people again. All because I said "Yes."

You never know where opportunities will come from, so give your best effort to the work in front of you (except for porn) and trust that the people around you are paying attention.

12

When the Door Is Ajar, Push It Open

After the success of *Space Jam*, there was a happy convergence of my growing skills and a demand for those skills. DreamWorks SKG was getting off the ground with ambitious plans for an animated film studio. I got called to work on a quirky little movie called *Shrek* as an additional editor. The primary editor had the final responsibility for decisions, and I shared the workload and became part of the creative team.

Shrek was probably the most successful movie I have been a part of, but you'd never know it from the time I was there. We worked in rented offices across from a used car lot, as the DreamWorks studio campus was still being built. When it rained, the roof leaked, and we had to cover our computers with plastic sheeting to avoid the risk of short circuits and electrocution. The story was based on a six-page illustrated children's book, and we struggled to find the spine of a movie story in those thin pages. At one point, Shrek was living at home with his parents, and there was a witch character, but they didn't stick. One thing after another seemed to go against us, so it's something of a miracle that the movie got finished and turned out to be so successful.

The lesson learned as we spun our wheels for months and months:

Trust the process.

Stay positive and give your best, no matter how dire the circumstances. You never know what may happen.

RISKS AND REWARDS

Being an additional editor was a step up, and I felt thrilled to be working at a brand-new studio with sky high expectations. But the role became stale after a while because I wanted to test the ceiling of my own capabilities. Could I handle the stress and responsibility of being a lead Editor? I was looking for a new challenge.

This came in the feathered form of *Chicken Run*, an animated feature produced at Aardman Animations in Bristol, England. At that time, there were no editors in the UK familiar with the DreamWorks way of working (intense and demanding), and producers were looking for someone willing to travel.

I met with Michael Rose, one of the Aardman producers in LA and he suggested I go to Bristol for a few months to get them up and running. I countered by offering to relocate for the whole run of the show if I could take the lead editor role. A suggestion as natural as flowing water, the offer came out of my mouth and sat there between us as a living thing that could solve both our problems. It would be a turning point in my working life. After some further back and forth, we agreed to undertake this leap of faith.

With only two-weeks-notice, I flew to Bristol to take up a new upgraded position. I had two weeks to wrap up my life in Los Angeles, negotiate working terms, pack up the house with my pregnant wife, Madi, and exit the contract we just signed to buy a new house. We would undertake the upheaval of moving to a new country where we had no family, knew hardly anyone and where our first child would soon be born.

Was I crazy to take such a risk?

Why would I do such a thing?

The feels. It just felt right.

I knew in my bones that this was a golden opportunity and I managed to convince my very brave wife that this leap of faith would land us in a better place. I was 41 years old.

Turns out, I was right.

Chicken Run was probably the best experience of my editing career. In a series of fortunate events, the people were great to work with, the movie was endearing, and the audience and critics loved it.

I remain proud of what we achieved. After all the stress of how I got involved, my first movie as lead editor was a big success with a London premiere on Leicester Square. To top it off, our daughter, Zelda, was born a happy and healthy *Chicken Run* baby.

MARK SOLOMON

Ginger
"Listen. We'll either die free chickens or we die trying."
Babs
"Are those the only choices?"

13

Loyalty and Trust

I had become an established freelance editor with a real credit on a successful movie, but it struck me almost immediately that the playing field had changed. I was no longer a fresh-faced additional editor who could help in a crunch. Now, I was competing for jobs with lead editors who had more experience and many more credits. I had entered a new competitive arena and didn't have a map of how to handle it. Political savvy was something I hadn't paid enough attention to, and now I saw how important it was. With strong allies and solid relationships, you stand a much better chance of succeeding.

FINDING YOUR TRIBE

We grow with our allies over time. For example, the producer you forged a good relationship with becomes a studio executive who can greenlight projects. The director you shared a foxhole with on a scrappy independent film becomes a big name who wants allies they can trust as their projects and budgets grow larger. That's why building relationships is so important!

Everyone likes to work with people they know and trust. You will find your own tribe of colleagues who share common values, tastes, and experiences. If you're lucky, you move with the tribe and strengthen the bonds from project to project.

How do you find your tribe? For me, it meant becoming the ally I wanted to find. By setting a standard of respect and integrity, it becomes a value that guided my decisions in hiring assistants and how to treat them. My aim was to be a *mensch* and attract colleagues who felt the same way. If you don't already know, *mensch* is a Yiddish word that translates roughly as a "true gentleman" who is honest, loyal, and held in high regard.

The well-respected film producer and executive Ted Hope advocates for building a better culture in moviemaking by doing the right thing even when it's difficult. By rewarding good behavior, some of the less honorable ways of Hollywood lose currency. I agree with Ted 100 percent. It's up to us to make things better.

Freelancers are vulnerable to the whims of skittish executives who are notoriously overpaid and insecure, and you can expect to see mystifying decisions because of fear, self-protection, or a twisted expression of their idea of power. But if you can count on your tribe to pick you up when you fall, you can thrive in the freelance arena for the long haul.

FRESH EYES (A WORD OF CAUTION)

If you're ever in a meeting and an executive says that the movie might need "fresh eyes" on it—beware. "Fresh eyes" is code for "we have lost confidence in you and think it's time we bring in someone new."

You are now caught in the crosshairs and could be fired at any moment. Your self-confidence is vital, so radiate a sense of calm certainty about the best way forward, which you can articulate with passion and clarity. Sometimes, it works.

In an ideal world, you work on projects with people you like and trust. Depending on the demands of your monthly cash flow, that's not always possible. You may have to accept a position that's not a great fit.

Freelance life is like a game of musical chairs. When the music stops, you must find an empty seat. But when you're raising a family, your impulse to take an exciting job out of town, or to accept a discounted fee to work with a new hotshot director, becomes a family decision.

Things change, but don't get discouraged. A good fit is out there.

REFERRALS

In the beginning, your challenge is to survive in the freelance desert with no connections and no credits, scratching out an opportunity before you die of thirst in the blazing heat. Once you get past that stage, you wriggle your way in as a freelancer and start moving from job to job. You build connections and get referrals from former colleagues. It starts to feel like you've got momentum. That's when the challenges change.

Referrals are essential to a freelance work life. Naturally, you want to work with people you know and trust. Most people do. Building relationships with talented, creative co-workers is good for everyone. When a position opens that's right for you, as it did for me on *Space Jam*, you hope your name will be put forward.

A referral is something you can offer, too. When a desperate, frazzled producer asks if you know somebody who can do a job, it bodes well for you if you can name someone who has the right skills to meet the challenge. If the person you recommend does a brilliant job, their shine reflects well on you. You become recognized as someone who is well-connected and a valuable resource for solving problems. Always a good thing.

Casting actors is related. Sometimes, voice talent on an animated movie is difficult to pin down. Ideally, you want someone who can play the role convincingly *and* attract attention with their social media profile. On *The Tale of Despereaux*, we struggled to find the right voice for Princess Pea, until one day the name Emma Watson popped into my head. The actress and the role suddenly fit together like a lovely hand in a wizard's glove. She helped the movie, and by suggesting her name, I upped my value to the production.

If, on the other hand, you recommend someone who isn't up to the job, or even worse, causes problems for the producers or the studio, that won't look good for you. Referrals have currency and will influence your social standing in the community, both positively and negatively. Before you volunteer one of your buddies for a job opening, give some thought to how that might play out. Do you have confidence in your friend's ability? Are they a good fit for the skills needed and will their personality mesh with the other people involved? It isn't an exact science, but putting some thought into your referrals is wise.

This also applies to you. When someone recommends you for a job, your ability to deliver reflects not only on you, but the person who referred you. The relationships you build, the friends and allies you make, are a big part of freelance life. Nurture those relationships by being honest and trustworthy, and always give your best effort. That way, you can build an organic social network of cooperation and mutual trust.

All for one and one for all.

HOLD YOUR NERVE

If you're ambitious, you will want to advance quickly and knock down walls to embrace greater opportunities. But once you've done everything you can to land a plum position or agree on a contract, or you're waiting because the ball is in someone else's court, the best course of action may be to stay still and wait. Don't push or follow up. Wait and see how the cards land and proceed from there. It takes a lot of inner calm to pull this off, but it can be an effective way to demonstrate your suitability in a volatile, freewheeling business.

I had my eye on *The Tale of Despereaux* because it meant moving my family from Los Angeles to London, which was appealing for several reasons. I met with the producers, which went well, and then I heard nothing for a couple weeks. I resisted the urge to follow up because I didn't think it would help. Feeling confident that I was the best candidate for the job, I tried not to think about it too much and the phone eventually rang. Waiting was the best course of action, to hold my nerve.

As a freelancer, how you handle stress is important to your long-term health and wellbeing. If you can relax your expectations and not become attached to one particular result, you will be happier in the long run and become a better colleague and collaborator as you move from project to project.

It's entirely possible that you were born under a lucky star, but you should accept the likelihood of meeting disappointments at some point. We all do. An exciting project can collapse for lack of finance or because of scheduling conflicts or a million other reasons. Fairly or unfairly, you may get fired from a project or be undermined by negative chatter. Rise above the offscreen drama and keep your eye on the prize—to deliver a compelling visual story that audiences will remember. The rest fades from memory.

14

When All Else Fails, Embrace Uncertainty

Every freelancer hits a slow patch, when no one returns your calls, texts go unanswered, and your finances start bumping ominously against your credit limit. You may become suspicious of Google algorithms and curse the inventor of text messaging. I know I have.

Consider a tongue-in-cheek suggestion to buy nonrefundable tickets. What sense does that make? Hear me out. The way I figure it, if you commit to paying for something you'd really enjoy, such as an exotic vacation or tickets to a show, surely a plum job offer will come along that forces you to reconsider and ruin your plans. Forget that trip to Tahiti. Maybe next year.

(Your results may vary!)

Considering the pressures to solve story problems, keep your collaborators happy and navigate the vicissitudes of freelance work, how do you keep *yourself* healthy and positive?

If this is your chosen field, what can you do to keep from losing your passion for movies and storytelling? A hobby might help, and an understanding family certainly will, but the wisest counsellor you can rely on is looking at you in the mirror.

It's time to dig a little deeper.

PLAY THE PART

One time, I was called to work on a Sunday morning. Bleary-eyed, I dragged myself to the basement cutting room to spend my day off in front of the screen. I knew it had to be done and that I would be spending time with our writer/producer, a filmmaker I admired. We had things to figure out, and this was our only chance given the pressure of our schedule.

Once I got everything up and running a few minutes later, in he walked. He dropped his bag, took a slug of coffee, and slapped me on the shoulder, staring at my screen as a rueful smile crossed his face.

"This is the life we have chosen."

He was quoting *The Godfather: Part II*[46] when the Lee Strasberg character, Hyman Roth, tells Al Pacino about life in the gangster business. I don't think making films is a criminal enterprise, but it does take commitment, and if that means coming to work on a Sunday morning, or agreeing to some other outlandish demand, so be it. You're a professional. Play the part.

---

[46] *The Godfather Part II* (1974) Screenplay: Mario Puzo and Francis Ford Coppola. Director: Francis Ford Coppola. Editors: Barry Malkin, Richard Marks, and Peter Zinner.

DECLARE VICTORY AND MOVE ON

We may as well talk about getting fired. It's a part of freelance life that can seem cruel and senseless, but you might as well think of it as a rite of passage because sooner or later the "hook" comes for everyone.

I got fired from my first paying job as an assistant editor in New York. I got fired from my first job back in L.A., even after the success of *Chicken Run*. I got fired from my first job in London and from my last job in Montreal. It happens.

Now, to be sure, some of these firings were just the natural ending point of an assignment that came earlier than expected. Some were a surprise, and some were a relief. Some hurt a lot.

I learned that the best course of action is to treat getting "released" as a learning experience and to let go of any negative emotion attached to the process.

Be grateful for the lessons learned and move on.

Holding on to resentment or replaying arguments in your head does you no good at all. Declaring victory means seeing the positive in what you gained from relationships with colleagues, what you learned about the craft of storytelling, and the insights about yourself. Moving on means letting go of any baggage or attachments so you can free yourself to be ready to face your next challenge.

EMBRACE UNCERTAINTY

As a creative freelancer, you face a life of uncertainty. As an editor, you adapt to changes in the culture, in the business and within yourself. You may as well learn to embrace that. When a project is completed, your job is finished, too, and you'll need to find the next one. Even with a job, you never know when financing disappears, writers go on strike, or a pandemic shuts down production. There is a high level of uncertainty in this line of work and it's not for everybody. But the rewards are satisfying, both personally and creatively.

Learning to live with uncertainty is not all bad, as you gain life skills and learn to see the epic dimension of everyday life. Learning to keep your balance as you ride the highs and lows will sustain you emotionally in multiple aspects of your life.

As for a high, I did get a glimpse of the summit once. After co-editing *Frankenweenie*, a Tim Burton movie about a boy who brings his dog back from the dead, I was exhausted and needed time to recover. Long, long days, and a brutal commute to an industrial neighborhood had worn me down.

While relaxing at home in London, I got a call from a colleague to congratulate me on being nominated for the 2012 ACE award for editing an animated feature. An honorary society, the American Cinema Editors, hold an annual awards gala to recognize the best editing achievements of the previous year.

I was stunned. My work on *Frankenweenie* had been a very positive experience, but I hadn't been nominated for an award before and the possibility wasn't on my radar.

Cut to a few weeks later.

I'm in Beverly Hills with a tuxedo bag over my shoulder, heading into the Four Seasons Hotel for a two-night stay, courtesy of Walt Disney Studios, which financed *Frankenweenie*. The gala dinner was held in a ballroom at the Beverly Hilton, with formal clothes, a master of ceremonies and a long evening of handing out statuettes in the various categories.

To risk repeating a cliche, it was an honor just to be nominated. I felt very fortunate to be present in a big room with top professionals in my field. All the best editors were there, many supported by their spouses and their directors and producers. Steven Spielberg sat at a table with his longtime editor, Michael Kahn. Director David O. Russell was there to support his *Silver Linings Playbook*[47] editors, Jay Cassidy, and Crispin Struthers. Walter Murch, the eminent film and sound editor, held forth in a corner of the room. I was proud to share a table with my co-editor, Chris Lebenzon, and our producer, Allison Abbate.

I could play the jaded cynic and scoff at the whole scene, but there was a such a feeling of fellowship in that room, a respect for the contribution of editing to the moviemaking enterprise, and a celebration of editors telling a visual story. I was thrilled. Experiencing an evening like that was a reward by itself.

Despite the ups and downs of a freelance life, some stories *do* have a happy ending.

---

[47] *Silver Linings Playbook* (2012) Screenplay: David O. Russell and Matthew Quick. Director: David O. Russell. Editors: Jay Cassidy and Crispin Struthers.

REEL 3
Outtakes

1. What you know about storytelling won't matter if you can't get hired.

2. An alternative way to find helpful allies is to look to older generations, people who have years of experience and aren't competing with you to get a foot in the door.

3. As a freelancer, how you look for work demonstrates how you will do the job.

4. Once you schedule a meeting, scan for news about the person you are about to meet.

5. Negotiation is a valuable skill to develop. It's important to get the terms right, because most every job has rough patches that range from uncomfortable to excruciating.

6. Once you get your foot in the door with a working credit or two, figure out how to advance. Once you're hired, become a valuable crew member. Attitude counts.

7. Be choosy. One of the powers you have as a freelancer is the power to say "No" to projects you don't want to be associated with—under any circumstances.

8. You never know where opportunities come from, so give your best effort and trust that the people around you are paying attention. Trust the process. Stay positive and give your best, no matter how dire the circumstances. You never know what may happen.

9. Freelance life is like a game of musical chairs. Things change, but don't get discouraged. A good fit is out there. Referrals are essential to a freelance work life.

10. As a freelancer, how you handle stress is important to your long-term health and wellbeing.
Despite the ups and downs of a freelance life, some stories *do* have a happy ending.

"Don't edit from knowledge; edit from feeling."
—*Michael Kahn*

REEL 4

Facing the Mirror

Facing the Mirror

Your own story is a hero's story. Embrace the dramatic arc and see the raw material of your day-to-day experience as an epic tale of mythic dimension.

Consider what Joseph Campbell said in *The Hero with a Thousand Faces.*

"The journey of the hero is about the courage to seek the depths; . . . the uncanny discovery that the seeker is the mystery which the seeker seeks to know."

Learn to see setbacks and disappointments as necessary bumps on the path to eventual triumph. They may cause pain in the moment but will make for a better story to tell in the end.

15

Your Creative Process

As a film editor, you are the first audience for the scenes in progress and you need to watch as a first-time viewer would and be as open and receptive as you possibly can. It takes courage to let yourself be moved emotionally.

What specifically does the scene make you feel?

What does the scene want to be?

Do you notice unspoken subtleties in the performances that could open new layers of emotion?

If you develop that intention further, will the result be more vivid and memorable, or would it tip over into sentimentality and feel false?

Let the images and the story live inside you, as it's a months-long process and the characters and the rhythm will take on a life of their own. Depending on the material, this can be unpleasant, but it must be done.

Editing takes a total commitment to reach the deepest layer of emotions. Your focus must always be to get the best from the material at hand. Giving yourself to the process is an essential requirement of the job. You're not the only one feeling it, of course. The director and producers, if they're any good, feel the same as you do, and there's a meshing of sensibilities that you must be willing to engage.

Along with being open emotionally, it helps to be able to talk persuasively about those feelings. This isn't always easy, and many editors fall back on 'this way just feels better,' but the ability to name and describe the feelings that arise will help your collaborators think more clearly about the material and offers a vocabulary to focus on subtleties of feeling and adding nuance.

It's like if you ever read a book and your teacher asks you about it. "I liked it" or "It was good" won't cut it. *Why* did you like it? *What* (specifically) made it good?

EMOTION AND INTUITION

Paul Hirsch, the editor of *Star Wars*[48], once said, "Film editor is not just a job; it's being a host organism."

This is true for a lot of creative work. What I think Paul was getting at is that you must bring more than your professionalism and craft to the job. It calls for you to exercise your inner resources. You need to engage your intuition and

---

[48] *Star Wars* (1977) Screenplay: George Lucas. Director: George Lucas. Editors: Richard Chew, Paul Hirsch, and Marcia Lewis.

your emotions to bring a story to life, as I mentioned in the *Preview*.

OVERCOMING RESISTANCE

There will be days when despite every intention and effort, ideas just don't come, and you feel stuck. It's a natural part of the creative process, and I can share some tools to help get you through it.

Become aware of seemingly unrelated thoughts and feelings that bubble up while you are working on a scene. Is it possibly a cloaked message for something you can use? If you suddenly feel a new sympathy for a character, pay attention to that. Are they more complex than you first thought? Can you tease something out of their performance to add a layer of humanity and empathy in the audience? Does a reshuffling of scenes offer unexpected interest?

There's value in happy accidents, so allow the random in.

As you work along, trying to make order from the chaos of all that material, don't forget to welcome happy accidents. Pay attention to these seemingly random juxtapositions that yield a fresh moment of clarity. This can be how a new piece of music goes with the picture or the way two unexpected images create a moment of surprise or humor. On many projects, each moment of screen time is so controlled and worked over that the result feels labored, and a breath of fresh air and spontaneity is decidedly welcome.

Let it in.

Come up with a daily practice to keep yourself centered and aware. Write morning pages, practice yoga, or go for a run.

Something like meditation or mindfulness will nurture your serenity and calm. It will expand your inner resources and benefit not only yourself; it will also make your work environment a calm, welcoming space where colleagues feel free to explore creative possibilities with you. It's a good sign if creatively 'the room where it happens' is *your* room. You can encourage that with your positive attitude and openness to new ideas.

YOUR BALANCING ACT

Work/life balance has been mentioned before, but over the long run, it's important to maintain a healthy balance between your working life and your personal life or you will wind up exhausted and burned out. In the beginning, the demands of the job can be seen as glamorous, thrilling and a test of your resolve to succeed. But after a few years of meeting intense demands, it starts to feel like you are being exploited, and you find the need to look after your whole self. The job will always be demanding, and while you're working, it can be impossible to find the time to socialize, spend time in nature, or whatever you do to feel like yourself.

Try to look at a longer horizon. You may not find much personal time within the work week, but over the course of a year, or between jobs, you can create the time to do what feeds you most.

It can take a few years to find the best rhythm for a healthy freelance life. Learn to be patient with yourself. You'll get there. Even during the heaviest work week, you can find little pockets of time to replenish your inner resources. Walk around the block; go to a church on your lunch hour to meditate or schedule a massage. Whatever gives you a feeling of peace and lowers your stress levels. That way, you avoid being driven to respond to the latest crisis and learn to play the long game and keep your self-awareness intact. You will be happier, and as a result, you will become a more valuable co-creator.

16

Meeting the Muse

There is not a single best way to contact your muse for creative guidance. You will find your own method if you look for it. What I *can* tell you is the way it works for me, and you can determine what resonates or inspires something similar in you.

When I struggle to solve a creative problem, rather than give up in frustration, I call upon my muse and see if there's another way to go about it.

Here are three imaginative exercises to help you contact your muse.

1. Start by giving your muse a character, based on someone real or imagined. Pick someone you admire creatively and who has your best interest at heart. Write out a dialog between yourself and this muse, asking for help and listening for an inner response. In a spirit of improvisation, say "Yes" to whatever inner prompts arise and fine-tune the signal

as you go along. Let yourself be surprised by whatever bubbles up.

2. In your mind's eye, go with your muse to the beach with a bucket and shovel to dig in the sand. Be aware of the sound of the surf, the heat of the sun, and how the sand feels between your toes. Dig with the intention to find something that helps to solve the creative problem you're facing. Dig until you find something and then bring it up to the surface. You can talk to your muse about it or just handle it with the intention to understand how it can help you.

3. Imagine that your muse is waiting for you at the top of a hill on a bright, sunny day. You climb up the hill with a question in mind. Feel the effort of walking up the path. Imagine the flowers and trees that you pass, how the temperature cools as you climb higher. Then arrive at the top, where your muse welcomes you to admire the view. You sit down and ask your question, listening with your inner ear for an answer. After talking for a while, thank your muse and go back down the hill.

These are suggestions to stimulate your imagination to work with your muse. Try a few, see what works best, and adapt as necessary.

By practicing with these inner tools—being open emotionally, looking for random solutions, refining your intuition and working with your muse—you will develop a resilience in the face of creative blocks. Insecurity won't seem as daunting or troubling. You will know how to handle anything that comes your way. You got this.

ABOVE THE LINE WITH WRINKLES

In 2004, I was editing a live-action feature on the Universal Studios lot for a new independent company run by a group of ambitious young producers. The script was fun, but the project's appeal for me was working with a company passionate to produce movies. I was happy to work with them and see what opportunities might arise. I would go out to the bar with the team after work and learned to enjoy Maker's Mark bourbon. Still do.

The working environment was positive, and I could see they wanted to produce quality movies, even though their only completed movie was a vicious martial arts movie with little to commend it. But this was Hollywood. Scripts came pouring through the front door and one of them had my name on it. It was a Filipino movie about a grandmas' beauty pageant. The roles were cast with stars from Manila who wanted a chance to impress a wider audience. The script was amusing and quirky and it was handed to me to get my approach on how I would direct it. This was, in my eyes, a golden opportunity.

This was at a time soon after *My Big Fat Greek Wedding*[49] had been a surprise hit and lots of countries with domestic film businesses believed they could reproduce that success. The script for *Wrinkles* (which never got made!) had charm and humor, which I thought I could adapt for North American tastes.

---

[49] *My Big Fat Greek Wedding* (2002) Screenplay: Nia Vardalos. Director: Joel Zwick. Editor: Mia Goldman.

Two related problems arose. One, was finding actors who could believably play Filipinos *and* have the name recognition to attract film distributors, and the second was raising enough money to get the production underway.

I gave them my take on the script. My pitch was that with an editor's eye I could shoot economically and make the most of our limited budget. After some further discussion, I reached out for a golden handshake and my shot at the director's chair. I was so thrilled I wandered round the Universal lot in a happy daze thinking about how to make the most of this big chance. I saw Mel Gibson outside a soundstage and felt a powerful urge to run up and tell him the good news.

The next few weeks were a whirlwind of location scouting, casting, and production meetings to fill out the key creative roles. What an exciting time! I was flown to Manila to meet the cast, and I organized a table read to get all the actors together to read through the script and imagine how it would play as a movie. I was impressed with their professionalism and commitment to the project. We held a rehearsal to get a sense of how we would work together, and my theatre experience came in handy. We spoke the same language. A photo was staged with the cast—all smiles, pen in hands, signing their contracts. Everything looking rosy.

Back in L.A., we carried on with casting to fill out the smaller roles and wracked our brains to find some bankable names who could pass for Filipino and help us attract investors. I went with our lead actor to a fitting at the huge costume warehouse on the Universal lot and that's when it started to hit me: *I'm going to direct a real movie.*

Working together with the screenwriter, our script showed signs of polish, so I had storyboards drawn up to guide the more complicated scenes. Everything seemed ready to start principal photography. One week to go.

Then, the soap bubble popped.

Our investors decided to pull out, and production ground to a halt. The production office shut down and we never recovered. For months after, we looked to regroup, recasting and shuffling locations around to save money. We enlisted the support of the Filipino community in southern California who were enthusiastic to support the project, but it never came together.

A glimpse of Hollywood glamour, then suddenly, it was gone like a mirage. The whole experience was thrilling but ended in such huge disappointment. I felt devastated for weeks.

So, what can you learn from this sad tale?

Motto: "Declare Victory and Move On."

Sometimes, the best course of action is to stop fighting, gather your resources and leave the field of battle. Take whatever lessons you can learn from the experience and point yourself toward the future. You develop a tougher skin dealing with disappointments and your resilience becomes a badge of honor.

SOHO REVELATION

What did I move on to? The opportunities that attracted me were working as a teacher and consultant, helping producers with animated movies that needed tightening or teaching film students looking for a career in movies.

The most vivid memory was from my last day teaching in the UK. I had been leading a short course in film editing at the METFilm school in London and wanted to finish the term with a tour of post-production facilities in Soho, giving students a firsthand look at a major filmmaking hub.

I arranged a tour of two different facilities where I had worked on previous projects and could call in a favor.

It was a magical day, sharing my love for filmmaking with enthusiastic young students who could begin to imagine themselves working in a professional creative environment. The first studio laid out the red carpet, treating my students like potential clients (which they were) and showing clips of award-winning films the studio had recently worked on. Famous actors passed through the lobby, and we had the thrill of entering a buzzing creative hub.

Luck was with me, as Adrian Rhodes, the sound mixer from *Chicken Run,* happened to be working on the mix stage. We held an impromptu Q & A to reminisce and answer questions from students about our work together. A short walk down memory lane let students see the mutual respect and camaraderie that Adrian and I shared. That goes to the heart of what makes moviemaking such a fulfilling, collaborative experience.

On the second tour, we saw clips of Oscar-winning films, asked lots of questions and met various professionals working at their craft. At the end of a long day, I stood with a circle of energized students outside on the streets of Soho. They were buzzing about their possible futures.

Before splitting up to choose a pub, I reached out to shake hands with one of my students and they all spontaneously gathered to form a circle and acknowledge our time together by shaking my hand. I could feel a real connection of gratitude that flowed between each one of us, and as I walked away, I felt a wave of deep emotion.

I had shared what I loved and the value of passing on my experience had been acknowledged. I realized at that moment that I was fulfilling the promise made in my "letter to the editors" many years before—to pass on what I had learned.

That moment was so full. I felt honored to find an opportunity to work with movies and storytelling and grateful and exhilarated to share what I knew.

And now I share it with you, over my shoulder.

A WORD ABOUT TECHNOLOGY

When you start out in a field where the technology is constantly changing, you may feel discouraged by how much you don't know. But what seems like an obstacle can be a great competitive advantage. Yes, you're new and your inexperience means you don't have a vast storehouse of knowledge. This also means you have less outdated material that needs to be forgotten. You are automatically at the front of the curve because legacy solutions no longer apply. All you must learn are the newest, most current solutions instead of comparing with the past and letting go of how it used to be.

Since AI is the new shiny thing, why not embrace it with both hands? You're now in the same position as everyone else, learning how it works for the first time. You don't have to forget anything or let go of old habits. You'll absorb it quicker and are more likely to innovate and discover capabilities that others may not see.

You're new, so embrace the newest tech. Use your underdog superpower. For example, you can view AI as a tool to help and support you. You may ask, how can AI help an aspiring film editor?

Here are a few ways AI can assist you in your journey:

Automated video editing:

AI-powered software can analyze and process large amounts of footage, making it easier to sort, organize, and select the best shots. This can save you time and effort in the editing process.

Enhanced creativity:

AI tools can suggest creative ideas and provide inspiration for editing techniques. They can analyze patterns in successful films and offer suggestions on how to improve your own work.

Efficient post-production:

AI can automate repetitive tasks, such as color correction, noise reduction, and image stabilization. This allows you to focus more on the creative aspects of editing and deliver high-quality results even faster.

Smart content analysis:

AI algorithms can analyze the content of your footage, which makes it easier to search for specific scenes, objects, or even emotions. This can be particularly useful when working on large-scale projects with extensive footage.

Real-time collaboration:

AI-powered collaboration tools enable multiple editors to work on the same project simultaneously, regardless of their physical location. This streamlines the editing process and promotes efficient teamwork.

AI is a tool that can enhance your skills and creativity as a film editor. It's important to embrace it as a complement to your expertise and not as a replacement.

IT'S A WRAP

If you previously felt confused and anxious about pursuing a career as an editor, now you have the storytelling chops to deliver the goods of a well-told story. You have a practical map of the territory as a creative freelancer, and you have explored the inner resources you can bring to achieve creative success and keep an even keel. Now, go and make the most of it.

Remember what you found here: feature the good stuff and hide the rest. If you run into trouble, declare victory, and move on. And when the opportunity arises, add something of your own so that when your time comes, you will know the reward of passing on your story to the next generation.

REEL 4
Outtakes

1. Your own story is a hero's story. Embrace the dramatic arc and see the raw material of your day-to-day experience as an epic tale of mythic dimension.

2. Learn to see setbacks and disappointments as necessary bumps on the path to eventual triumph. They may cause pain in the moment but will make for a better story to tell in the end.

3. As the editor, you are the first audience for the scenes in progress and you need to watch as a first-time viewer would and be as open and receptive as you possibly can.

4. Editing takes a total commitment to reach the deepest layer of emotions. Your focus must always be to get the best from the material at hand.

5. As you work along, trying to make order from the chaos of all that material, don't forget to welcome happy accidents.

6. Create a daily practice to keep yourself centered and aware. Write morning pages, practice yoga, or go for a run.

7. It's important to maintain a healthy balance between your working life and your personal life or you will wind up exhausted and burned out.

8. It can take a few years to find the best rhythm for a healthy freelance life. Learn to be patient with yourself.

9. You're new, so embrace the newest tech. Use your underdog superpower.

"The most enjoyable part of directing or filmmaking for me is editing. It is literally the language of filmmaking. It is right there, and you learn constantly how dumb you are and how much you have to learn every time you take a picture into the cutting room."
—*William Friedkin*

Acknowledgments

Many people contributed to the completion of this book, and I owe them my gratitude. Maria Constantides has been a loyal confidant since the start, and a great source of encouragement.

My thanks to Steve Patoine. Julia McCarthy, Clay DeHart and Dominic Searles for their valuable feedback and answers to my questions. I hope this finished version will serve you as visual storytellers and talented editors.

To Allison Abbate, Susan Van Allen, Mario Canki, Stephen Ringold, Jay Stuart, Marie Claire Lalancette, Suzanne Pretten, Lili Cledenning, Brian Dunnigan, Rob Kobrin, Brian Powell, Leslie Hough, Hank Rosenfeld and Thom Dean for reading and offering sound counsel.

Thanks to Claire Winters for pointing me in the right direction, Jim Kammerud for the illustrations, and David Tabatsky, who worked his magic as a book editor and made this process fun.

To Joel Solomon, for design help, technical support, and a great turkey dinner.

And to Zelda Solomon, a fine writer and an extraordinary young woman. She's the reason I started this adventure in the first place.

Love you, Z.

About the Author

Mark Solomon is a visual storyteller with a memorable body of work in animated movies. His cut his teeth as a film editor on *Space Jam* in 1996 and went on to edit some of the most highly regarded films of the past three decades. *Shrek*, *Chicken Run*, and *Frankenweenie* are among his award-winning highlights.

He also edited *Scoob! Holiday Haunt, SGT. STUBBY: An American Hero, Sherlock Gnomes, The Tale of Despereaux, The Fox and the Hound 2, Unbeatable Harold, Shark Tale, Stuart Little 2, Escape from Planet Earth, Dalmatians 2: Patch's London Adventure,* and *Spirit: Stallion of the Cimarron.*

As a producer and writer, Mark's projects have taken him from the Himalayas in Nepal to the Olympic Stadium in London. He is a recognized expert, consulting on international productions, including *Ella Bella Bingo* (Norway), *Condorito* (Peru), *Googly* (Scotland), *Simon's Cat* (UK), and *Rumbuck and Spink* (Australia).

His work spans all the major Hollywood studios, generating more than $1 billion worldwide for a global audience in 30 different languages.

He has been honored for his work on *Frankenweenie*, nominated for best editing of an animated feature film, A.C.E. Eddy and Best Animated Feature (Oscar), and *Chicken Run*, nominated for best picture (Golden Globe).

To support future filmmakers, Mark has taught at film schools and universities in the U.S. and the United Kingdom, and he continues to enjoy creative collaborations on projects large and small.

Over The Shoulder represents his first adventure into the world of books and publishing. Enjoy!

www.7pinespublishing.com

A Final Note ...

Hey there, fabulous reader! If you think this book dropped some storytelling gems, why not hop over to Amazon to leave a review? Your words might be just the nudge someone needs to dive into *Over the Shoulder* and join the party! So please spread the love and let's make this book the talk of the town!

Thank you from deep in my writer's heart!

CREATE A KINDLE REVIEW
https://www.amazon.com/review/create-review/?ie=UTF8&channel=glance-detail&asin=B0CSXW35L5

CREATE A PAPERBACK REVIEW
https://www.amazon.com/review/create-review/?ie=UTF8&channel=glance-detail&asin=B0CT3JD12D